Beckett Great Sports Heroes

Wayne Gretzky

By the staff of Beckett Publications

House of Collectibles • New York

LY

H This is a registered trademark of Random House, Inc.

Published by: House of Collectibles
201 East 50th Street
New York, NY 10022

Distributed by Ballantine Books, a division of Random House, Inc., New York,
and simultaneously in Canada by Random House of Canada Limited, Toronto.

Manufactured in the United States of America
ISBN: 0-676-60032-8

Cover design by Michaelis & Carpelis Design Associates, Inc.

Cover photo by Scott Levy of Bruce Bennett Studios

First Edition: August 1996

10   9   8   7   6   5   4   3   2   1

The Publisher would like to thank Dr. James Beckett
and the staff of Beckett Publications for providing the editorial and photo content of this book.

Managing Editor Rudy J. Klancnik and Art Director Jeff Stanton had the able editorial, design and production assistance of
Barbara Barry, Rob Barry, Therese Bellar, Amy Brougher, Emily Camp, Belinda Cross, Randy Cummings, Marlon DePaula, Eric Evans, Barbara Faraldo,
Mary Gonzalez-Davis, Tracy Hackler, Brent Hawkins, Paul Kerutis, Benedito Leme, Sara Leeman, Lori Lindsey, Sara Maneval, Louis Marroquin, Mike McAllister,
Lisa McQuilkin Monaghan, Daniel Moscoso Jr., Randy Mosty, Lisa O'Neill, Mike Pagel, Mike Payne, Tim Polzer, Reed Poole, Will Pry, Fred Reed III,
Susan Sainz, Evan Salituro, Gary Santaniello, Judi Smalling, Doug Williams, Steve Wilson and Mark Zeske.

Additionally, the Publisher would like to acknowledge the entire staff of Beckett Publications, which was instrumental in the completion of this book: Dana Alecknavage,
Jeff Amano, Jeff Anthony, Kelly Atkins, Claire Backus, Kaye Ball, Airey Baringer, Randy Barning, Eric Best, Julie Binion, Louise Bird, Pat Blandford, Marco Brizuela, Bob Brown,
Chris Calandro, Randall Calvert, Mary Campana, Susan Catka, Jud Chappell, Albert Chavez, Theo Chen, Marty Click, Gary Coleman, Andres Costilla, Lauren Drewes, Ben Ecklar,
Denise Ellison, Craig Ferris, Gean Paul Figari, Jeany Finch, Carol Fowler, Joe Galindo, Gayle Gasperin, Stephen Genusa, Loretta Gibbs, Marcelo Gomes de Souza,
Rosanna Gonzalez-Olaechea, Duane Green, Jeff Greer, Mary Gregory, Robert Gregory, Jenifer Grellhesl, Julie Grove, Patti Harris, Mark Hartley, Mark Harwell, Beth Harwell,
Pepper Hastings, Joanna Hayden, Chris Hellem, Melissa Herzog, Dan Hitt, Mike Jaspersen, Jay Johnson, Steven Judd, Eddie Kelly, Wendy Kizer, Rich Klein, Brian Kosley, Tom Layberger,
Jane Ann Layton, Stanley Lira, Kirk Lockhart, John Marshall, Teri McGahey, Omar Mediano, Beverly Mills, Sherry Monday, Mila Morante, Mike Moss, Allan Muir, Hugh Murphy,
Shawn Murphy, Mike Obert, Stacy Olivieri, Wendy Pallugna, Laura Patterson, Gabriel Rangel, Bob Richardson, Tina Riojas, Grant Sandground, David Schneider, Christine Seibert,
Brett Setter, Dave Sliepka, Sheri Smith, Rob Springs, Margaret Steele, Marcia Stoesz, Phaedra Strecher, Dawn Sturgeon, Doree Tate and Jim Tereschuk.

15.00

Foreword

The Great One

Never has a nickname more effectively captured a player's essence

AP / WIDE WORLD PHOTOS

Power Rangers Gretzky and Messier can't wait to drop the puck on '96-97.

There are cool nicknames such as Prime Time (Deion Sanders) and The Kid (Ken Griffey Jr.).

There are hallowed nicknames such as The Sultan of Swat (Babe Ruth) and The Rocket (Maurice Richard).

There even are nicknames that take the place of a player's real name such as Penny (Anfernee Hardaway) and Magic (Earvin Johnson).

But if you're looking for the best nickname ever, look no further than The Great One, a.k.a. Wayne Gretzky.

Wow, The Great One. Now that's a nickname that says it all. Thanks to alliteration, Gretzky and Great effortlessly roll off the tongue. Thanks to Gretzky's spectacular performances for the last two decades, The Great One fits like a snug pair of skates.

No player in any sport has changed the game or rewritten the record books more thoroughly than The Great One. All-time leading goal scorer, all-time leader in points, all-time leader in assists, etc., etc. You get the picture. Heck, even the title of this book, *Beckett Great Sports Heroes*, is perfect for Wayne's world.

Now as Wayne's remarkable career takes one final shift change, he finds himself alongside good friend and former teammate Mark Messier and in a city that boasts a pretty fair nickname in its own right.

How The Great One does in The Big Apple is anyone's guess. Let's go out on the limb and just assume there's something *great* on the horizon.

Rudy J. Klancnik
Managing Editor

CONTENTS

Front Cover Photo by Scott Levy / BBS
Special Thanks to Bruce Bennett Studios for its photo contributions.

KEN LEVINE / ALLSPORT USA

BEYOND
Greatness

Wayne Gretzky has dominated, influenced and transcended his sport as only a rare few athletes ever have done before. Now, in the twilight of his career, The Great One's passion for victory has been reignited by his reunion with Mark Messier.

U ntil Wayne Gretzky came along, we didn't know how great great could be. We really had no clue.

Every time an athlete excelled to a higher degree or achieved a feat faster than before, we simply exulted. We crawled along under the false assump-

BY JAY GREENBERG

tion that humans were exactly that — limited — never understanding we were measuring the universe with a pocket ruler. This isn't to suggest that efforts to expand sporting achievement weren't noble, but Gretzky has taught us that they also were relatively pathetic.

Consider:

Gretzky's 92 goals in 1981-82 topped Phil Esposito's previous record by 16, and his 212 points that season eclipsed Esposito's old mark by 60. Gretzky's 163 assists in 1985-86 surpassed Bobby Orr's standard by 61.

With such numbers, The Great One has made the incredible entirely credible. The sheer scope and prolific nature of his feats so overwhelm those of his peers that calling him merely the greatest hockey player ever damns him with faint praise. Gordie Howe needed 26 seasons to establish NHL records of 1,850 points and 801 goals. Gretzky broke the points record in his 11th season and the goal mark in his 15th.

Further:

• Gretzky won eight of his nine Hart trophies consecutively. Only Bobby Orr ever won as many as three in a row.

• Gretzky's 10 scoring titles give him four more than Howe ever claimed, five more than Esposito and six more than Stan Mikita.

• Gretzky holds or shares 61 NHL records, a number so staggering, it tends to blur his signal achievements.

Picture Hank Aaron as not only baseball's all-time home run leader, but its single-season homer king and all-time hits leader as well. That's Gretzky's place in hockey.

Sentimentalists and puck-drunk ex-goalies rationalize Wayne's Gretzgantuan numbers, citing the dilution of talent and the evolution of a different style of play. They cling to the nonsensical belief that somebody actually outplayed Gretzky during the course of an NHL career.

Such a conclusion stretches the bounds of credulity. Orr revolutionized the way defense could be played and established significantly higher statistical standards for excellence at that position. It can be argued that Orr carried the puck more than Gretzky and broke up a lot of rushes, making him a more effective all-around player than The Great One. But Orr's career, cut drastically short by knee injuries, produced just 915 points. Orr's 1.39 points per game average is dwarfed even by Mario Lemieux's 2.05, let alone Gretzky's 2.08.

Unquestionably, Howe played the majority of his career in a much tighter checking era. But the fact that jobs were more competitive in the six-team league doesn't necessarily mean the level of play was, too.

The kinescopes don't lie about the slower pace of the pre-expansion NHL. If stick handling, as the old-timers lament,

B. BENNETT / B. BENNETT STUDIOS

has diminished as an art form, it's because today's players have less time and space to hold on to the puck. Current players pass just as skillfully as the old-timers and most shoot harder and skate faster. Bigger, faster and better athletes, and the influx of European- and American-born players, make today's NHL just as competitive — but higher scoring — than the pre-expansion league.

This isn't suggesting that Howe — skilled, strong, durable, and inordinately graceful both on and off the ice — ever will be known as anything less than Mr. Hockey. Or that circumstances, not merely statistics, must be considered

when comparing two great players from different times. But all things considered, only in longevity does Howe surpass Gretzky. Take it from an unimpeachable source: Gretzky stands alone.

"He's good, and I know because I played with him," Howe once said. "If you want to tell me he's the greatest play-

er of all time, I have no argument at all."

No one does. Not reasonably. Not remotely.

Not only has Gretzky obliterated the previous standards of excellence in his sport, but the ratio of improvement,

One of Gretzky's many gifts is his deft scoring touch, honed through years of practice.

applied to records in other team sports, reveals the staggering nature of his achievements.

The Elias Sports Bureau has deter-

Though immortalized through a statue outside Northlands Coliseum in Edmonton, Gretzky remains a star people can relate to.

magnetism helped baseball recover from a betting scandal and inspired the building of a stadium twice the size of others of that era. He was the dominant player on baseball's dominant team, winning four World Series and seven American League pennants.

The impact of Gretzky's performance and personality upon his sport rivals Ruth's.

Gretzky's stylistic contributions to a game may be unprecedented. Unlike legends of other sports and other times, his gift is neither speed nor power. His is creativity. Michael Jordan, Larry Bird and Magic Johnson may or may not have seen nine other players on the floor better than Bob Cousy did. But unlike

Gretzky, they didn't obliterate assist records.

Arguably, Gretzky also developed a greater sense of foresight and anticipation than any skater before him. Only Gretzky has flourished from behind the goal, or created more opportunities out of less space, or more regularly arrived where the puck inevitably wound up.

His artistry has mirrored his importance to his sport. Gretzky, who signed with the World Hockey Association at age 17, before he was eligible for the NHL draft, was an important factor in making the older league interested in a merger. Five years later, he legitimized the 1979 merger by leading one of the former WHA clubs to a Stanley Cup.

mined his 212 goals in 1981-82 are the equivalent of 85 home runs — 24 more than Roger Maris hit in 1961; a 2,941-yard NFL rushing season (Eric Dickerson holds the record with 2,105 in 1984) or 67 touchdown passes by a quarterback (Dan Marino holds the standard at 48, also in '84). Wilt Chamberlain dwarfed previous NBA scoring leaders, but arguments raged during his day as to whether he or Bill Russell was the more dominant player.

A case can be made that no one ever has done in any sport what Gretzky has accomplished in hockey. And when you consider the wider impact of one player's career upon a sport, only Babe Ruth ranks with Gretzky.

In hitting 59 home runs with a livelier ball in 1921 and raising the record by a staggering 25, Ruth also drastically elevated standards of excellence and excitement. The Babe, too, was the object of a blockbuster transaction: The Red Sox sold him to the Yankees for $100,000 and a $300,000 loan. His

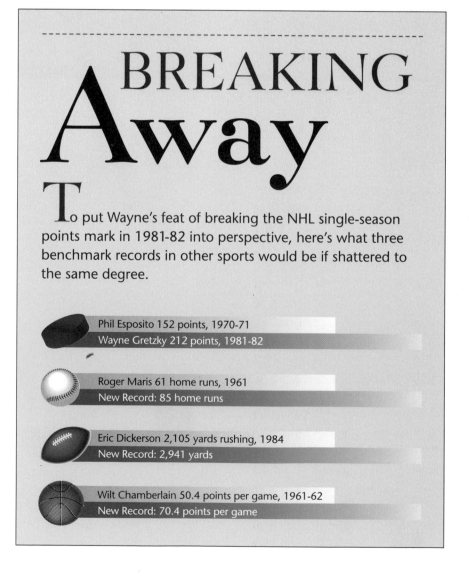

A BREAKING Away

To put Wayne's feat of breaking the NHL single-season points mark in 1981-82 into perspective, here's what three benchmark records in other sports would be if shattered to the same degree.

Phil Esposito 152 points, 1970-71
Wayne Gretzky 212 points, 1981-82

Roger Maris 61 home runs, 1961
New Record: 85 home runs

Eric Dickerson 2,105 yards rushing, 1984
New Record: 2,941 yards

Wilt Chamberlain 50.4 points per game, 1961-62
New Record: 70.4 points per game

After winning four Cups in five seasons, Gretzky, like Ruth, became the object of one of the most astonishing and expensive transactions in sports history. The $15 million, five-player, three-draft choice extravaganza in 1988 that landed Gretzky in Los Angeles not only energized an endangered franchise in the nation's second-largest market, but keyed a popularity explosion for hockey in California (San Jose, Anaheim) and the Sun Belt (Tampa, Miami, Dallas).

As Gretzky approaches the twilight of his career in New York, there remains no greater presence in any sport. No heir has emerged to Jordan — perhaps the most compelling basketball player ever (but not vastly superior statistically to either his contemporaries or to the standard bearers of another

era). Baseball's marketers fret about the absence of one transcendent personality. The greatest NFL legend, Joe Montana, recently reached the end of his career, and the next round of heroes (Troy Aikman? Emmitt Smith?) have the ability, but may lack Montana's charisma.

Mike Tyson spent three years in prison — like other superior athletes of our generation, a victim of self-destruction. Gretzky, on the other hand, rarely has had a hair out of place.

Oh, he has thrown an occasional snit about critisicm (which generally is mild) and sometimes complains about trying to fill the responsibilities of being Wayne Gretzky and still having a family life. At times, he even has rebelled from those obligations. Gretzky didn't show up at the NHL Awards presentation in 1988 when Lemieux dethroned him as

Despite the burdens inherent in being his sport's designated spokesman, Wayne's accommodating nature and candor have earned him leaguewide respect.

Most Valuable Player, and he slept in through a sold-out All-Star workout in Pittsburgh in 1990.

Considering the burden of being all things to all people, considering the innuendo suggesting he had managerial influence with the Kings, considering what Canadians perceive as his defection from his native Canada when he agreed to the trade from Edmonton, Gretzky has suffered amazingly few backbites during the course of his career. He's exceedingly thoughtful of his teammates and rarely ducks a postgame press conference, a sick child (time per-

Even the Gipper, aka Ronald Reagan, turned out for Gretzky's lone title bid with the Kings.

mitting) or any issue affecting the game.

"Thank God he is the person he is," Colleen Howe, Gordie's wife, has said, "because Wayne is bigger than the league."

Despite Gretzky's stature, regardless of the off-ice obligations his fame brings, hockey — not celebrity — remains his passion. Even at age 35, despite all his accomplishments, he retains a becoming insecurity about continually having to re-prove himself.

Gretzky's resurgence from the back problems that caused him to miss 39 games of the 1992-93 season carried the Kings that spring to upset playoff victories over the Flames and Canucks. But when his merely average start to the Cup semifinals against Toronto drew mediocre reviews, Gretzky's response said everything about what he has done and who he remains.

He was genuinely hurt by one column in a Toronto paper that, correctly yet tamely, suggested he had been ordinary in the series to that point. "I stuck it in my pocket and took it home with me on the plane," he said later. "Maybe those kinds of things get me going.

"I'm under a lot more pressure than anybody in this game. I don't think Mario has the pressure I do. I don't think Eric Lindros does either.

"When you accomplish something, everybody wants to see you do it again and again. You do whatever you can to motivate yourself. And I put pressure on myself to prove people wrong.

"My whole life has been that way," Gretzky continues. "When I was 10, I was too small. At 17, I was too slow. I wasn't a 'great' player until I won a Cup. I went to L.A. and then it was, 'You haven't done anything in L.A.' If I hadn't succeeded in the last series [against Vancouver], it would have been because I was 32 years

When Gretzky leaves the ice for the last time, he'll leave a legacy as a champion, a sportsman and the holder of virtually every NHL scoring record.

old and lost my drive.

"My numbers are so high, people don't believe them, so I'm always being challenged to do them again."

He still thrives on that challenge. Gretzky scored the overtime game winner in Game 6 of that series against Toronto in 1993, then registered three goals and four points in the Kings' Game 7 victory.

If, after 17 years of watching him uncannily rise to occasions such as that one, we still are surprised by how truly great great can be, the grandest definition of the word is Wayne Gretzky's ongoing passion to show us.   •

Jay Greenberg is a columnist for the New York Post.

Wayne Gretzky has traveled an eventful path. As a youth,

he reluctantly endured the intrusive spotlight attracted

by his wondrous hockey skills. In Edmonton, his scoring

exploits and role in four Stanley Cups carved a niche for him as a civic

treasure. Following a stunning trade to Los Angeles in

1988, he found himself enjoying a wider platform and

gracefully assumed the role of preeminent ambassador for

his sport. The 10 pages that begin on page 16 retrace the

steps that took Gretzky from child star to hockey legend.

By Tim Wharnsby, Jim Matheson and Rick Sadowski

ICEcapade

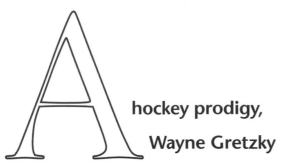

A hockey prodigy, Wayne Gretzky learned early about the benefits and burdens of athletic fame

"I always felt like I was the happiest kid in Canada. Until I was about 12. That's when I realized I was the unhappiest."

— *Wayne Gretzky*

Young athletes love to dream.

Young hockey players dream about becoming the next No. 99.

But do these dreamers really fancy the childhood that was heaped upon Wayne Gretzky?

His youth indeed differed from that of his peers. Sure, sometimes it was fun and exciting. But, at times, it also was restrictive and overbearing. Newspapers carried stories about him at age 6. Wayne was signing autographs at age 10, the same year he was the subject of a national magazine article. By age 13, he had hired an agent.

At 14, Wayne left his home and family in Brantford, Ontario, to play Junior B hockey 90 minutes away in Toronto. A 30-minute national television show featuring him appeared a year later.

"I always felt like I was the happiest kid in Canada," says Gretzky. "Until I was about 12. That's when I realized I was the unhappiest."

The happy period began when his father, Walter, flooded the backyard during the winter. Wayne began skating at age 2 and spent every spare moment, day and night, skating around like a loose puck on the rink they called the Wally Coliseum.

As a 6-year-old, Gretzky received a tryout and impressed the coaching staff of the Brantford Nadrofsky

novice (age 10-and-under) team. The age disparity between Wayne and his teammates became apparent when he received his uniform.

"I was a puny 6, which meant the sweaters they had for the players looked like ballroom drapes on me," Gretzky recalls in his autobiography. "My sweater was so big, it was constantly getting caught on my stick on my shooting side. One day my dad tucked the shooting side into my pants, and it's been there ever since."

Playing against boys mostly aged 10, Wayne managed only one goal in his first season in 1967-68. A defenseman at the time, the boy wonder improved quickly. Wayne's goals total increased from 27 to 104 to 196 the next three seasons

"Wayne is a wonderful little hockey player," his coach, Bob Hockin, remarked at the time. "He ends up being more of a team player than most people realize. I know that some say he plays too often, but every time he's out there he's a threat because he controls the game."

In 1971-72, his fifth season with the novice Nadrofsky club, a 4-4, 11-year-old Gretzky achieved

Wayne was so far ahead of his peers that when he scored 378 goals in '71-72, he won the scoring race by 238 goals.

The jealousy and resentment he encountered often made Wayne's youth hockey days far from carefree.

greatness for the first time, amassing a whopping 378 goals in just 69 games.

That incredible season earned him "The Great Gretzky" moniker from *London Free Press* sportswriter John Herbert and placed him under the microscope for good. Posters at arenas trumpeted a future Gretzky visit.

He signed autographs for his fellow students at school. At games, the attention was unbearable. He often sent his best friend and teammate, former Detroit Red Wings netminder Greg Stefan, out to sign autographs for him. Stefan and Gretzky would exchange team jackets. One problem emerged, however: Stefan often signed the autographs "Gretsky."

The spotlight also meant fabricated or exaggerated stories about the Gordie Howe wanna-be. One story that wasn't imagined is that Gretzky's idol was — and still is — Howe. Gretzky went as far as getting his hair cut like Mr. Hockey. Howe and Gretzky would develop a friendly relationship down the road. But their first meeting came when Gretzky was 11.

"What do I work on?" Gretzky asked.

"Work on your backhand, because the defense-

CANAPRESS PHOTO SERVICE

men in the league force you to your backhand. It doesn't jeopardize your opportunities," Howe replied.

Hockey wasn't the only sport at which Wayne

excelled as a kid. He also enjoyed some success playing lacrosse and baseball. On the diamond, Gretzky was a pitcher, shortstop and third baseman.

The furthest his baseball career traveled was playing for the Brantford Red Sox of

the Inter-County Major League, a high-level senior league in Southern Ontario.

The repeat World Series champion Toronto Blue Jays even liked what they saw in Gretzky. They offered him a tryout during the summer of 1980, the summer following

Gretzky's first season in the NHL.

"They asked me to come out, throw the ball and field a little," Gretzky says. "I liked baseball so much, but I couldn't throw hockey away. If I could have, I would have done both."

After his 378-goal season, Gretzky played two years of pee wee and a season of bantam in Brantford. He scored 391 more goals during those three years, but most of the time he was miserable. The attention, jealousy and backbiting eventually drove him from his hometown.

Encouraged by current Los Angeles Kings general manager Sam McMaster,

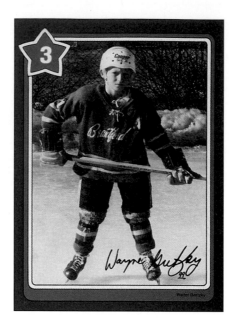

The 1982-83 Neilson's Gretzky #3 captures Wayne at his "home" rink — the backyard Wally Coliseum in Brantford.

Wayne went off to Toronto to play Junior B hockey for the Seneca Nats at age 14. The Ontario Minor Hockey Association protested, contending the move violated residence rules. But Gretzky eventually was allowed to play.

"It was so silly that I was 14 and had to leave my house and family because I excelled as an athlete," says Gretzky, who moved to Toronto to escape the wrath of other parents in Brantford who believed the hockey prodigy hogged the puck from their kids.

In May 1977, Gretzky was selected third overall in the major junior draft by Sault Ste. Marie, which is about 11 hours north of Toronto. Gretzky lasted until the third pick because the teams that drafted first and second, the Oshawa Generals and the then-Niagara Falls Flyers, respectively, believed Gretzky would perform in the OHL for only one season. They were right. Gretzky jumped to the World Hockey Association after one season in the Soo.

Gretzky enjoyed a boom year in his only full OHL sea-

son. He scored a league-record 70 goals, registered 182 points in 64 games (a rookie record that still stands), earned 1977-78 OHL Rookie of the Year honors and first donned his now famous No. 99.

Wayne wanted to wear Howe's No. 9, but the number was held by Brian Gualazzi. So, Gretzky started the season wearing No. 19, then later switched to No. 14.

Noting that New York Rangers Phil Esposito and Ken Hodge were wearing Nos. 77 and 88, respectively, Coach Muzz MacPherson suggested, "Why don't you try 99?" After initially rejecting the suggestion, Wayne donned No. 99.

The first night he wore No. 99, in Niagara Falls on Nov. 18, 1977, he scored three goals. "And after that, you couldn't have torn that number off me," Wayne says.

Ironically, the Soo is Phil and Tony Esposito's hometown. Gretzky eventually snapped Phil's record for most goals in a season. "I remember one day my dad phoned from Sault Ste. Marie," Espo says. " 'Hey, Phil,' he said, 'there's a kid here who is gonna break your record someday.' 'Yeah,' I said, 'Who?' 'He's called Gretzky,' my dad said. 'Geez, Phil, what a kid.' "

What a kid indeed. •

Tim Wharnsby is a sportswriter for the Toronto Sun.

Wonder Boy

Year	Team (League)	Goals
1967-68	Brantford Nadrofsky (Novice)	1
1968-69	Brantford Nadrofsky (Novice)	27
1969-70	Brantford Nadrofsky (Novice)	104
1970-71	Brantford Nadrofsky (Novice)	196
1971-72	Brantford Nadrofsky (Novice)	378
1972-73	Brantford Turkstra (Pee Wee)	105
1973-74	Brantford Turkstra (Pee Wee)	196
1974-75	Brantford Charkon (Bantam)	90
1975-76	Toronto Seneca Nats (Junior B)	27
1976-77	Toronto Seneca Nats (Junior B)	36
	Peterborough Petes (OHA)	0
1977-78	Sault Ste. Marie (OHA)	70

I n a boomtown on the Canadian prairie, Wayne Gretzky came of age as a person and a hockey superstar, having the time of his life in the process

"The first time I ever saw Wayne . . . I honestly thought he was one of the players' kids."
— *Glen Sather*

Back then, he was a different Wayne Gretzky than the hockey icon he is now. The number on his back read "99," but he was forever 18. He was an innocent babe who grew up to be hockey's Babe. His idea of heaven was playing 3-on-3 hockey games long after practices ended, with whomever was there.

Gretzky became an Edmonton Oiler in bizarre fashion. The saga began in June 1978, when he bid adieu to junior hockey (and his $75 a week salary) in Sault Ste. Marie and signed a $825,000 personal services contract with Vancouver entrepreneur Nelson Skalbania, owner of the WHA's Indianapolis Racers. Skalbania held the press conference in Edmonton. Gretzky walked down the stairs of Skalbania's Lear jet with a $50,000

FOCUS ON SPORTS

Wayne's exploits in Edmonton earned him increasing fame, such as when *Sports Illustrated* named him its 1982 Sportsman of the Year.

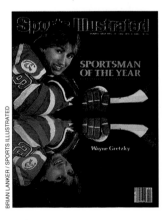

BRIAN LANKER / SPORTS ILLUSTRATED

Wayne and buddies Mark Messier and Paul Coffey played around in the locker room, but they were all business on the ice.

check in his hands representing the down payment on the contract, which he'd penned on the plane. "I wrote it on some school foolscap [composition paper]," said Gretzky, who still was in the 12th grade.

"If the [WHA] ever folds," Skalbania quipped, "maybe he'll just be a deckhand on my boat in the Mediterranean."

Five months later, the Indianapolis franchise failing, Skalbania traded Wayne to the Oilers, along with goalie Eddie Mio and forward Peter Driscoll. "Only 17 and already traded. Pretty funny," says Gretzky.

If Gretzky's hand shook while he signed his junior life away on Skalbania's plane, it may have been due to his surroundings. Wayne then had a fear of flying for

most of his time in Edmonton. He used to sit with his forehead resting on the back of the seat ahead of him on takeoffs and landings, his shirt drenched in sweat. It's the only thing he couldn't handle during his Oilers days, the only time he appeared human, like everybody else.

"That's it, I'm quitting," he often said, playfully, but with a hard edge to it. He tried hypnosis and several other treatments before his anxiety ended. Perhaps all the trips to the cockpit cured him. "Wayne, sit right down here and, by the way, could I please have your autograph?" was a more common request from the flight deck than "Please return your seats to the upright position."

"The first time I ever saw Wayne, at a morning skate in Indianapolis, I honestly thought he was one of the players' kids," admits former Edmonton coach Glen Sather. When Wayne scored

two goals that night, one on a shot from behind the net, the other a soft backhander through the goalie's legs, Sather had another thought: "We gotta get this kid."

Sather not only got Gretzky, he put him up until Wayne got settled. He stayed three weeks with Sather, his wife, Ann, and their two boys.

"Wayne was very naive and very young when he first got here, but he grew up in front of everybody," says Sather, who watched as Gretzky eventually owned the town but always maintained a semblance of privacy for himself. "He's been a superstar for 15 years, but he's still humble. He's never lost his roots or his humility. He's grown up to be probably the most mature, sensible superstar I've ever seen. He's never been a problem."

Gretzky received lots of help in his early Oilers days, particularly from savvy veterans such as winger Ace Bailey.

The only time Wayne nearly found himself in hot water, Ace bailed him out. Wayne and Ace had overslept their wake-up call one afternoon on the road and awoke at 6:40 p.m. for a 7:30 game. Bailey hustled the youngster into a cab, and Gretzky arrived at the rink a minute before the pregame skate. Bailey never made it to warm-ups, but was sitting drenched in his equipment in the room afterward. "Where've you been?"

Gretzky asked. Bailey had been in the shower, getting himself wet. "They never missed me," Bailey grinned.

You could never miss Gretzky in those heady days. Like the night in his second NHL season when he upstaged U.S. Olympic hero Jim Craig in Atlanta. Gretzky scored two dazzling goals and assisted on the winner in Edmonton's 5-4 comeback victory. "Craig had been saying some things," Gretzky explains. On one of his goals, Wayne changed hands on his stick — a "take that" gesture uncharacteristic of Gretzky.

The January 1984 night he extended his consecutive

point streak to 46 games typified the magic of those years in Edmonton. Gretzky knocked Troy Murray's waist-high pass out of the air with seven seconds left, then carried a Blackhawks' defenseman several agonizing feet before shoving the puck into the net with one second to go. "Wayne and empty nets . . . it's like a male dog in heat," says Sather, recalling the best of Gretzky's 46 career empty-netters.

"A broken bat single with two out and a full count in the bottom of the ninth," Gretzky laughs. "The fans booed when they pulled their goalie. When I scored, they booed even louder. That was the fun part."

Then there was the cold night in St. Louis in the early '80s when Gretzky scored on an amazing shot over Mike Liut's shoulder while taking a faceoff. He'd just learned that move from teammate Garry Unger. Wayne always was a quick study.

His years in Edmonton were a learning time for Gretzky. Everything was new. He was a kid, having the time of his life with best buddies Mark Messier and Kevin Lowe, who used to cook for Wayne at the downtown apartment they shared.

The three joked that they'd made a friendly wager about which one would get married first: Gretzky — who else? — won in 1988, when he married actress Janet Jones. Lowe later married Canadian Olympic double-medal skier Karen Percy. Messier remains single, but he has all of New York in love with him after leading the Rangers to their first Stanley Cup in 54 years.

Gretz, Mess and Lowe lived for a good time in Edmonton. Like in 1981, when they splish-splashed in the team's whirlpool, three men in a tub soaking in the glory of a stunning playoff upset of Montreal the night before.

Ten days later, Gretzky, Messier and Lowe were in Long Island playing the Stanley Cup champion Islanders. In Game 5, trailing three games to one in the series, they started singing like the Vienna Boys Choir with four minutes to go: "Here we go Oilers, here we go . . ." It underscored just how innocent No. 99 and his buddies were.

"I know it's high-schoolish, but we're all barely out of high school," reasoned Gretzky, who won the first of his 10 scoring titles that season. "We're the youngest team in the NHL, just a bunch of kids with nothing to lose."

Like most of us, Gretzky can't sing. He can't act either, lest you forget the episode of *The Young and the Restless* where he played "a hood from the Edmonton operation." Maybe if the show had enlisted tough guy Dave Semenko, the scene would have been more credible, but Gretzky always was willing to try things. That is, except for taking part in a "Fastest Gun in the West" story for the Edmonton Journal in the early '80s. "Not interested," Gretzky ducked. "I don't want people to know how hard my shot *isn't*."

The camaraderie shared and Cups won made for a magical time in Edmonton for Gretzky.

It never was as hard as those of Messier or linemate Jari Kurri, but nobody ever scored on more flip shots, flub shots and assorted backhanders. The goal that broke Phil Esposito's single-season goals record in 1982 illustrated Wayne's uncanny accuracy. Goal No. 77 was an off-balance 20-footer that squirted past Don Edwards in Buffalo with Goldie Hawn and Burt Reynolds in attendance.

Hawn and Reynolds were making a movie in Buffalo and staying at the same hotel as the Oilers. Before the game, their names alone appeared on the hotel's marquee. After Gretzky's record-breaking feat, the hotel added Gretzky's name. "Can you believe that? Burt and Goldie and me, together," remarked the wide-eyed youngster, who looked like it was Christmas morning posing for pictures after the historic goal.

Maybe Gretzky's gee-whiz attitude disappeared after he moved to Hollywood in 1988. After all, celebrities such as Sylvester Stallone, Kevin Costner and Tom Hanks frequently appeared in the Kings' dressing room. But in Edmonton, before The Trade, back in all his innocence, he was just one of the Boys on the Bus. The limo rides came later. •

Jim Matheson has covered the Oilers for the Edmonton Journal *since before Gretzky's arrival.*

Glory Days

Season	Club	GP	G	A	P
1978-79	Indianapolis	8	3	3	6
	Edmonton	72	43	61	104
1979-80	Edmonton	79	51	**86**	**137**
1980-81	Edmonton	80	55	**109**	**164**
1981-82	Edmonton	80	**92**	120	212
1982-83	Edmonton	80	**71**	125	196
1983-84	Edmonton	74	**87**	118	205
1984-85	Edmonton	80	73	**135**	**208**
1985-86	Edmonton	80	52	**163**	**215**
1986-87	Edmonton	79	**62**	121	**183**
1987-88	Edmonton	64	40	**109**	149

League Leader in Bold

I

n Los Angeles, The Great One may have performed his greatest feat yet. He energized a flagging franchise and sold the winter sport to sun-worshipping Southern Californians.

"The one thing I worried about was being a $15-million bust."
— *Wayne Gretzky*

The National Hockey League landed in Los Angeles in the fall of 1967, but hockey didn't really arrive until two decades later.

That's when, as if by providence, Wayne Gretzky suddenly appeared, and hockey in Southern California hasn't been the same since.

He showed up on the morning of Aug. 9, 1988, when the Kings and Edmonton Oilers consummated the most significant trade in hockey history. The deal that delivered No. 99 to the West Coast registered about a 9.9 on the Richter scale, producing aftershocks felt thousands of miles away in Canada, where a country mourned the loss of a national treasure.

"I kept asking myself, 'What can I do to try and make everybody pay attention to the team, to really stand up and take notice?' " remembers Bruce McNall, who as majority owner of the Kings engineered the blockbuster trade with Oilers owner Peter Pocklington. "I knew it would take something big for that to happen, but I never imagined Gretzky entering the picture. There's no question he has made it easier to sell the sport."

The Kings received Gretzky, who in the previous season led Edmonton to its fourth Stanley Cup in five years, forward Mike Krushelnyski and enforcer Marty McSorley in exchange for center Jimmy Carson, the rights to No. 1 draft pick Martin Gelinas, three first-round selections throughout a five-year period and $15 million in cash.

Gretzky's trip from the Great White North to the shores of the Pacific Ocean seemed a dream come true for long-suffering Kings fans, who at first might have thought reports of the deal were part of a cruel hoax.

Many of them squeezed into the ballroom of the Sheraton Plaza La Reina, near Los Angeles International Airport, for Gretzky's introductory news conference. A festive mood prevailed, with black-and-white streamers and balloons swaying from the rafters and music blaring out of loudspeakers.

The room erupted when McNall asked Gretzky to step to the podium and don a Kings sweater bearing the club's new black, silver and white colors. Contrary to popular belief, the decision to trash the old purple-and-gold uniforms was made months before Gretzky arrived.

"I remember that summer, I spent pretty much every day going to hockey clinics and doing interviews and et cetera and et cetera, trying to sell the game," Gretzky says. "It didn't happen overnight, and a lot of people put in a lot of hours. The one thing I worried about was being a $15-million bust."

The Kings' fortunes changed immediately. They improved 23 points in the standings, finished 11 games above .500 and advanced to the second round of the playoffs for the first time in six years. Gretzky, who scored the Kings' first goal of the season on his very first shot, shattered team records for assists (114) and points (168). So pervasive was his influence, he won the Hart Trophy as league MVP a record ninth time.

Gretzky made an equally impressive impact at the box office. Kings' season-ticket sales nearly tripled in just two years, climbing to about 12,000, a figure that remained constant. The team even turned a small profit in 1988-89, after it lost almost $5 million the year before.

Home attendance jumped from an average of 11,667 in the 16,005-seat Forum to a then-club-record 14,875 in Gretzky's first season. In 1991-92, the Kings became the only team in Los Angeles sports history to sell out every home game — even the chic Lakers never had done it. And even in 1993-94, despite a horrendous 27-45-12 record and failing to qualify for the playoffs in the Gretzky era, the Kings played to 98 percent capacity.

"I think it was important to get the first-time fans to come to our games," Gretzky reflects. "I think they found out how entertaining and exciting this game can be. We've come a long way in getting fans to come into our building. And I don't think they come for the hooligan aspect of the game. I think they come for the skating and the passing and the speed. I think they see hockey as an art form.

"And it really is a special thrill when I see people walking around town wearing Kings jackets and hats. It's kind of neat. It shows we do have a presence."

It's safe to say the NHL would not have welcomed two more California teams — the San Jose Sharks in 1991-92 and the Mighty Ducks of Anaheim in 1993 — if Gretzky hadn't been able to sell the sunglasses-and-shorts set on the sport.

During his eight years in Los Angeles, Gretzky not only bestowed credibility on a previously wobbly Kings franchise, he also played a pivotal role in reshaping the league as we know it today.

FOCUS ON SPORTS

Gretzky's celebrated arrival in Los Angeles in 1988 heralded a new era for the Kings.

The elevation of hockey from a sport with regional appeal in the United States to one embraced nationally likely wouldn't have occurred without his influence.

"I think people in the league were waiting to see what happened in L.A.," McNall says. "When they saw we were doing very well financially, they realized that putting more teams in California would be a natural. Obviously, Wayne's impact has been enormous. I knew his coming here would have a huge impact on the sport, but I honestly didn't believe it was going to be as big as it has become. Certainly, it turned into more than a simple hockey trade."

Gretzky also spearheaded the Kings' unlikely (and only) march to the Stanley Cup finals in 1992-93. This

Ice King

Season	Club	GP	G	A	P
1988-89	Los Angeles	78	54	114	168
1989-90	Los Angeles	73	40	**102**	**142**
1990-91	Los Angeles	78	41	**122**	**163**
1991-92	Los Angeles	74	31	**90**	121
1992-93	Los Angeles	45	16	49	65
1993-94	Los Angeles	81	38	**92**	**130**
1994-95	Los Angeles	48	11	37	48
1995-96	Los Angeles	62	15	66	81

despite missing the first half of that season with a herniated disk in his back that threatened his career and then suffering a serious rib injury in Los Angeles' playoff opener.

The Kings fell to Montreal in five games, losing three consecutive times in overtime. But they captured a new legion of fans, turned Hollywood into Hockeywood and provided beleaguered Los Angelenos a much-needed respite from news of riots, fires and other calamities.

The Kings couldn't sell out one game when the Forum opened 26 years earlier.

Now, fans purchased tickets from scalpers for $500 to watch Stanley Cup final games in a building warmed by sweltering June heat.

"These are exciting times," said Gretzky, who led all playoff scorers that year with 15 goals, 25 assists and 40 points in 24 games. "We take it for granted now that there will be 16,000 in our building every night when there used to be 8,000 or 9,000."

Gretzky generated excitement all by himself on March 23, 1994. In an otherwise meaningless game against Vancouver, The Great One became The Greatest One, breaking Gordie Howe's all-time NHL goals record by notching No. 802.

He now owns a hat trick of sorts: the NHL record for goals, assists (1,771) and points (2,608) — all in just 1,253 games.

Diplomat that he is, Gretzky avoided a spat with Howe during his march to the record. Howe, who scored 174 goals in six World Hockey Association seasons, claims that those goals should count toward the "professional record." Gretzky scored 46 goals in his only WHA season, thus leaving him 92 in arrears of

A cartoon in a local newspaper captured the predicament Gretzky faced in making hockey a hot topic in Southern California.

When's it ice over?

BRAMHALL
HERALD EXAMINER

Howe (975-883) according to this new math.

"Combining the NHL and the WHA . . . does that mean I can go back and win Rookie of the Year?" Gretzky jokes. He was referring to the NHL's edict that former WHA players were ineligible for Rookie of the Year honors when it absorbed four WHA teams for the 1979-80 campaign. Gretzky, then 18, scored 51 goals and 137 points in his inaugural NHL season.

"Where does it end?" Gretzky asks. "I know this record is for the NHL, and that's fine. If they want to put in an NHL record and a professional record for goals, that's fine, too."

Sadly, Gretzky doesn't have many years left in which to weave his magic and add to the league-record goals total he set in 1994. Most expect that his current contract with the New York Rangers will be his last.

Gretzky will be 36 years old during his 18th NHL season next year. And even though he wouldn't be completely satisfied with his career if he fails to win a Stanley Cup with the Rangers he's emphatic about

quitting before he no longer can meet his extraordinary personal standards.

Besides, he's financially secure, and eventually he'd like to spend more time with his wife and three young children.

"It's funny, but there were rumors I would quit once I got to 802 [goals]," Gretzky says. "But I'm going to keep going. I'd like to get 900 goals, 1,000 goals. I may not get there, but I keep thinking about it."

For a man who in just eight seasons reversed the fortunes of a franchise and led a league into a new era, what's not possible? •

Rick Sadowski covers the Kings for the Los Angeles Daily News.

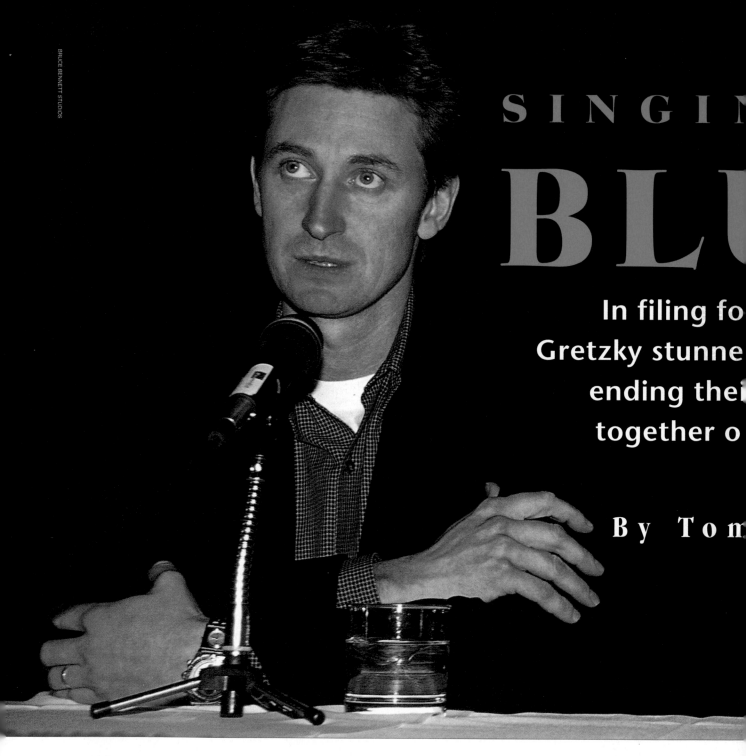

SINGIN

BLU

In filing fo
Gretzky stunne
ending thei
together o

By Tom

The Wayne Gretzky Era in Edmonton lasted 10 seasons and produced four Stanley Cups.

The Wayne Gretzky Era in Los Angeles lasted almost eight years and featured one trip to the Stanley Cup finals.

The Wayne Gretzky Era in St. Louis lasted four months and produced two playoff rounds.

On Feb. 27, 1996, the Blues traded a large chunk of their future for the game's most accomplished player. Four months later, Gretzky opted to become a free agent for the first time in his 18-season pro career.

In effect, the Blues rented No. 99 for 31 games. Despite suffering a con-

cussion and a back injury, Gretzky tallied eight goals and 13 assists in 18 regular season games. During St. Louis' 13-game playoff run, he registered two goals and — at the time — a league-best 14 assists.

Off the ice, Gretzky gave the Blues capacity crowds, front-page coverage, a run on No. 99 sweaters at the souvenir stands and a feel-good ending to what

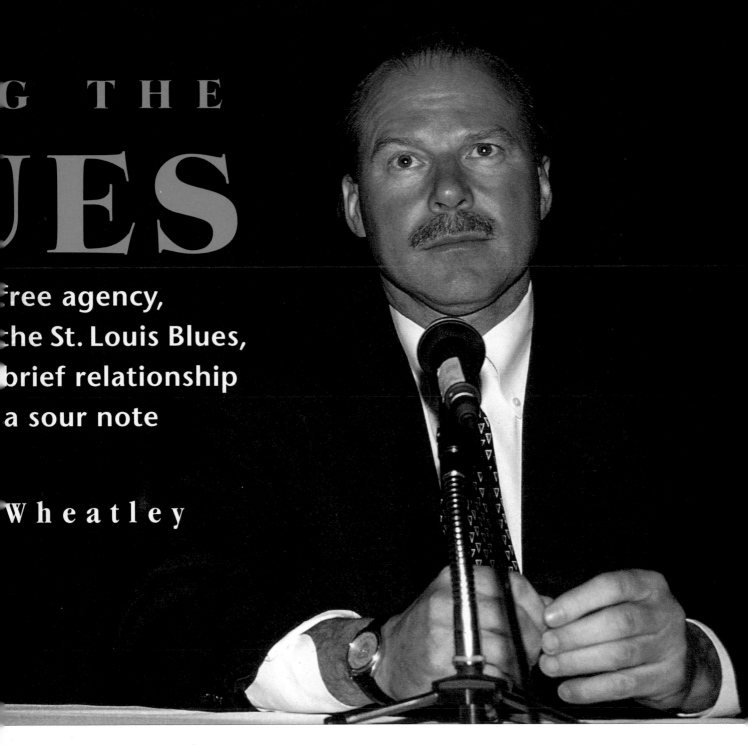

G THE
UES

free agency,
the St. Louis Blues,
brief relationship
a sour note

Wheatley

had been a dull, controversial season under head coach and general manager Mike Keenan.

The Great One arrived from Los Angeles amid much speculation and expectation.

At age 35, he had asked the Kings to make an immediate commitment to win or move him to a contender. Otherwise, Gretzky said, he would leave after the season as a free agent and the Kings would get nothing for him.

"I like to win," says Gretzky, who is not known for making controversial statements. "This is the first time I've ever stepped forward. People who know me say they've never seen this side of me.

"My gut was saying it's time to move on."

Differences of opinion kept Gretzky apart from Keenan, his coach for just 31 games.

So after several weeks of negotiations with several teams, Gretzky was traded to the Blues. In exchange, the Kings received three young forwards — speedy Craig Johnson, big Patrice Tardif and top prospect Roman Vopat — plus

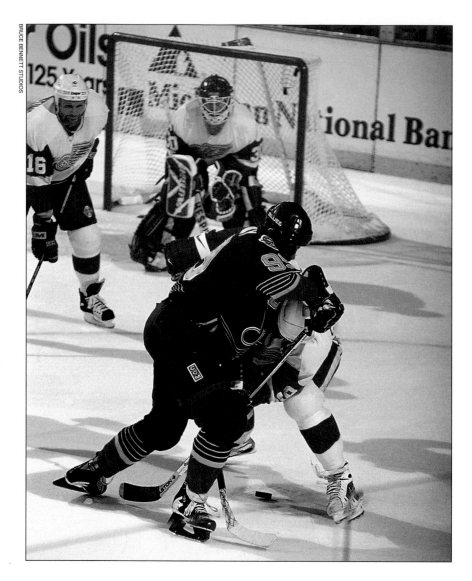

just from Gretzky's point of view.

Hull, after spending three days in mid-July at Gretzky's home in Los Angeles, said, "It's one in a million that he'd come [back]. It has nothing to do with money, no matter what they say about him testing the free agent market."

It was a much happier scene when his trade to St. Louis was announced.

"I look forward to a new start in St. Louis," Gretzky said at the time. "I

A Game 7 loss to Detroit proved to be Gretzky's last with Hull as a St. Louis teammate.

a fifth-round draft pick in 1996 and a No. 1 pick in the loaded 1997 draft.

Gretzky, whose wife grew up in St. Louis, said he looked forward to playing with the Blues for two reasons. He wanted to play with superstar winger Brett Hull. And he wanted to play for Keenan, his Team Canada coach for two championships in the Canada Cup.

At the end in St. Louis, Gretzky and Hull parted as friends. Gretzky reportedly left the Blues partly because they refused to issue a no-trade guarantee on Hull's status.

While never actually criticizing Keenan publicly, Gretzky was said to be turned off by Keenan's "Iron Mike"

coaching tactics.

In particular, after the Blues dropped the first two games of Round 2 in Detroit, Keenan ripped Gretzky in front of the team and then, publicly.

The Red Wings scored four goals during Wayne's first six shifts in an 8-3 loss in Game 2. Gretzky, who had two assists in the first two games, took full responsibility for those losses.

Coach Scotty Bowman and several Red Wings said that No. 99 seemed to be playing in pain. But if Gretzky's back was hurting him, he kept it to himself.

Later that night, Keenan went to Gretzky's hotel room and made an emotional apology.

But the damage was done, and not

am ecstatic about playing for Mike, and obviously it will be nice to have Brett Hull on my right side."

Gretzky held aloft a Blues sweater with his No. 99 on the back. It came complete with the captain's "C" on the front, surrendered gladly by Blues forward Shayne Corson.

"It's an honor to give the 'C' to the greatest player who's ever played the game," Corson says. "I don't care if I have an 'A' [as alternate captain]."

"You can have my 'A,'" Hull told Corson, who ended up with it. "I don't care. I just want him to get here. I've played with some of the worst centers

in the game, and now I get to play with the best one."

Gretzky joined the team for a practice in Vancouver that drew a spillover crowd of 2,000 fans.

Afterward, Hull said, "I'd be lying if I didn't say I'm pinching myself to see if this is real. He was sitting next to me on the bus to practice, and I thought back to all the bus rides I took where I was sitting in the back of the bus saying, 'I wish we could have someone like Wayne Gretzky.'

"Today, I thought that and I looked over and he's right there. I can't believe it."

Blues fans were even more excited. They moved Gretzky almost to tears with a thunderous ovation at his Kiel Center debut on March 5.

Gretzky repeatedly said that he loved St. Louis and its fans, and was confident that a long-term deal with the Blues would be worked out. He and his wife, the former Janet Jones, looked at more than 40 homes in the St. Louis area and even made a bid on one.

But Gretzky, through no fault of his own, may not have demonstrated his best hockey to his new fans and bosses.

On March 3 in Edmonton, in his second game with the Blues, he was

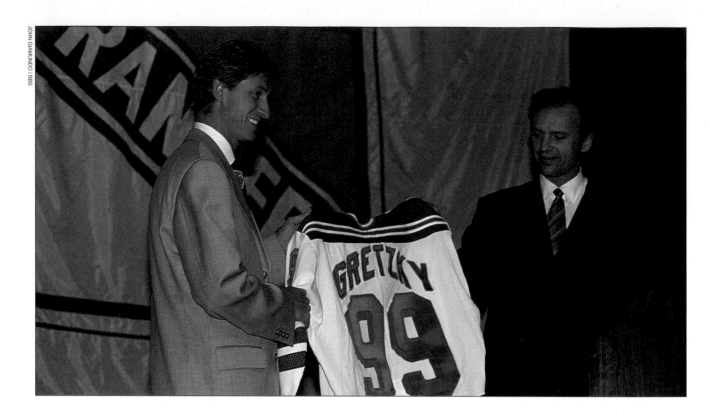

knocked down and almost out by an elbow from Oilers winger Kelly Buchberger. Gretzky left the game with a concussion but returned for the Blues' next game, his home debut.

Hull, who was used to having to create his own scoring chances, did not immediately click with The Great One. Hull scored seven goals in his first 13 games with Gretzky. Not a bad scoring pace, but it was no better than Hull had experienced before the trade.

The powerplay continued to struggle. Keenan, claiming Hull wasn't working hard enough, yanked him off Gretzky's line. Then, a string of injuries intervened.

Gretzky missed three games late in the season with a lower back bruise. Hull sat out four games with a muscle pull. Neither had fully recovered when the playoffs began.

Gretzky, always a shifty target seemed to be absorbing checks that he usually ducked. Fatigue may have been a factor. In Los Angeles, he logged about 15 minutes per game in the four-

line rotation of rookie coach Larry Robinson. Gretzky spent an average of 25 minutes on the ice per game under Keenan, who typically plays his best players relentlessly.

Against Toronto in Round 1 of the playoffs, Doug Gilmour nailed Gretzky with a body check. Even ponderous skaters such as Tie Domi caught the suddenly vulnerable Gretzky.

To Keenan, the Blues' medical staff and reporters, Gretzky insisted that he was fine. But he could not shoot with any zip, and he stepped gingerly onto the bench after every shift.

Gretzky's response after the Game 2 debacle with Detroit: "I'm not playing as well as I can. I can play better."

And he did. Finally clicking with Hull, Gretzky scored two goals — including a game winner — and two assists as the Blues won the next three games for a 3-2 series lead. But Gretzky managed only one assist as Detroit won the last two games and the series.

Following a Game 7 loss to Detroit,

It's doubtful Gretzky will look back with any remorse on his decision to sign with New York.

Keenan chose not to address the team after the season-ending loss. Two days later, Gretzky skipped Keenan's final team meeting to fly home to L.A.

Gretzky and his family had planned to move to St. Louis. Quietly, they withdrew their offer on a house, a subtle hint the Blues were not in his future.

The Blues continued to trumpet their last offer as the best Gretzky would get. But it became obvious that The Great One was not looking for a better deal, just an alternative to rejoining Keenan's team.

On July 21, Gretzky finalized that alternative by signing a two-year, $8 million contract with New York.

And so another Gretzky Era — short and bittersweet for The Great One and the Blues — came to an end as another dawned on the horizon.

Tom Wheatley covers the Blues for the St. Louis Post-Dispatch.

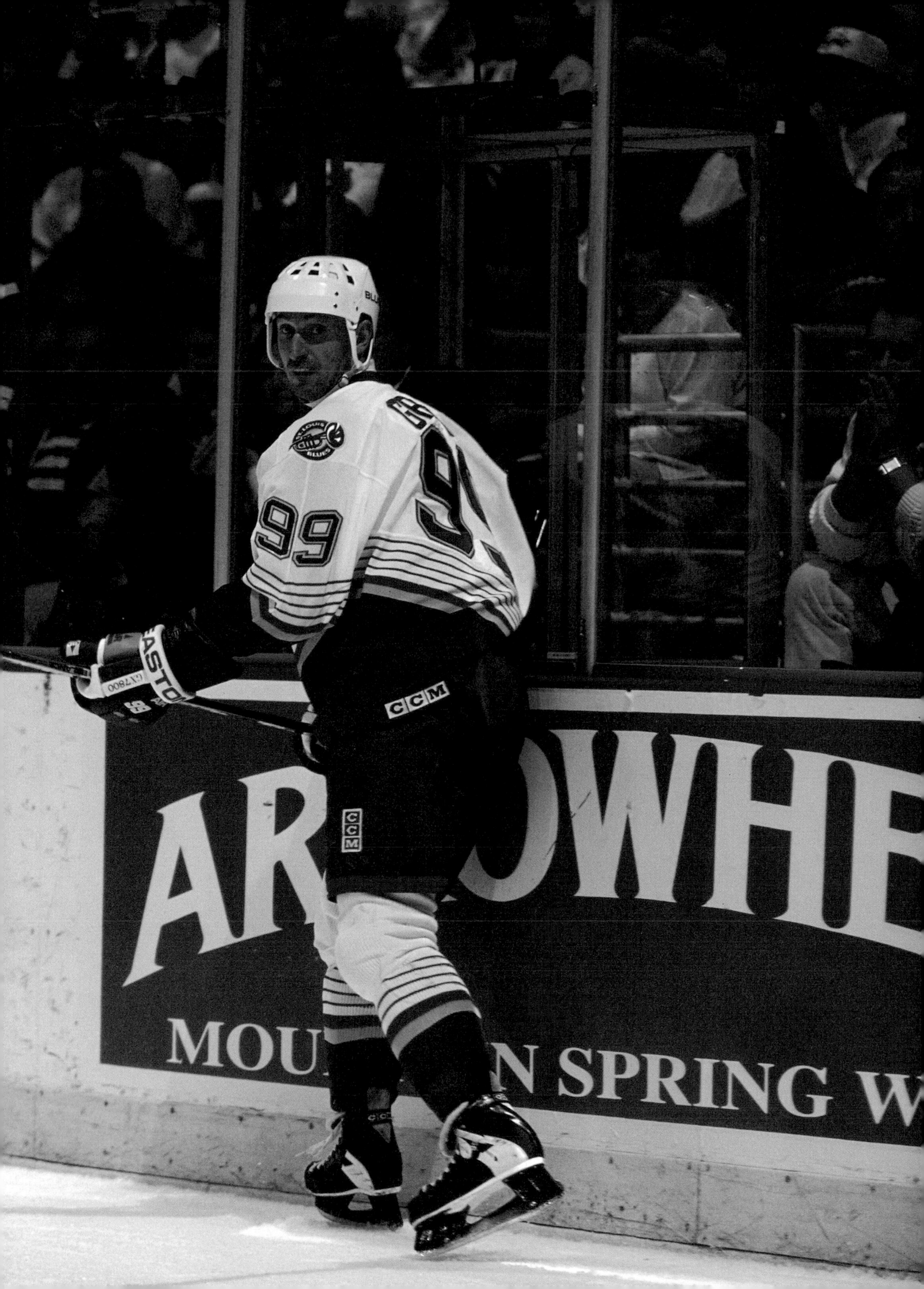
99
CCM
SPRING

By Cam Cole and Rick Sadowski

defining
MOMENTS

In a career studded with sparkling achievements, five moments in particular trace Wayne's rise to hockey icon

1 Four nights earlier, his total had stood at 41 goals in 37 games. He had a chance, pundits said, of beating the magical 50-goals-in-50-games record of Montreal's legendary Maurice "Rocket" Richard — equaled a year earlier by Mike Bossy. But any kind of small slump, and the chance would disappear.

Then, he had exploded with four goals against Los Angeles, and now, in the next game, he had rifled four more past Pete Peeters of the Flyers. As the final seconds ticked away, Philadelphia pulled Peeters in hopes of forging a 6-6 tie.

When the puck came to

**Dec. 30, 1981: goal
No. 50 in Game No. 39**

Gretzky, the 17,490 fans in Northlands Coliseum already had risen to their feet. The possibility of witnessing the impossible had been buzzing around the building like an electrical current ever since No. 99 scored his third goal of the game 3:54 into the second period. By that time, the Edmonton crowd — for the first time ever — had begun chanting "Gretz-ky! Gretz-ky! Gretz-ky!"

When Wayne slid a soft, 30-foot wrist shot into the empty net with three seconds left, he reacted as though he might leave his skin.

"It's the second-best feeling I've ever had — not quite as thrilling as beating Montreal in the playoffs last year," said Gretzky, who finished that season with 92 goals and 212 points.

He was at the height of his offensive powers, and the manner in which he had annihilated the Richard/Bossy benchmark left no room for any bleating by old-timers about how hockey was better in earlier times.

"All I can say is that I believe hockey is better now than, say, 15 years ago," Gretzky says. "The players are bigger and better than they were then — and 15 years from now, they'll be better than we are."

The hockey world had known Gretzky was great. Now, it acknowledged, perhaps for the first time, just how great he was.   •
— *Cam Cole*

CANAPRESS PHOTO SERVICE

2 The fans had come to boo The Great One in Calgary, where he was that city's most hated man, the most visible tormentor of the hometown Flames.

"I've been booed before," said Gretzky, "but here, they boo me like they really mean it."

But when Gretzky set up a goal by Pat Hughes 9:16 into the game to become the

March 25, 1982: The first player to break the 200-point barrier.

first player to reach 200 points in a season, the Calgary fans were drawn to their feet and into a standing ovation by the magnitude of the feat they had witnessed.

"It surprised me. I thought this was the last place this would ever happen," said Gretzky, who had been contemplating the improbable 200-point mark from the moment he broke Phil Esposito's single-season goals record the month before.

The question no longer was "Will he?" but "By how many?" Before the night ended, Gretzky would add another assist and two shorthanded goals.

Now, just 13 seasons after Espo had become hockey's first 100-point man, Gretzky doubled the gold standard. It had taken him 38 games to reach 100 points, 38 more to reach 200.

"It's like rushing for 3,000 yards or hitting 80 home runs in a season," Oilers assistant coach Billy Harris remarked.

"To me," said teammate Dave Lumley, "the fact that he's now got 90 goals is the unbelievable thing. And they say his shot can't break a pane of glass." •

— *Cam Cole*

3 He had won five cars, some 200 television sets and trophies galore for his individual virtuosity. But this night, Wayne Gretzky acquired the designation he wanted most of all: champion.

The youthful Oilers had been the consensus pick to win the Stanley Cup ever since their 1981 playoffs upset of Montreal. They stumbled in the 1982 playoffs, losing in the first round to the Los Angeles Kings. After scorching the league with 424 goals, they entered the 1983 playoffs as the overwhelming favorite. But the three-time defending cup champion New York Islanders blew them away in four straight in the finals.

In 1984, Gretzky and Mark Messier left no room for error. A more mature Oilers team, led by Messier's almost palpable will to win and Gretzky's machinelike production of 35 points in 19 playoff games, rebutted any questions regarding Edmonton's character. Outscoring the Islanders 19-6 in the final three games with Gretzky providing two goals in the clincher, the Oilers buried one dynasty and gave birth to another.

"It's exciting to win individual awards," said Gretzky, his eyes red from the cham-

May 19, 1984: Claiming his first Stanley Cup.

pagne dripping off his hair. "But there's no feeling like this. Nothing compares.

"I've been in the NHL five years, and all the time you pick up the paper and read, 'Well, they haven't won the Stanley Cup yet, so they're not that good.' We'll never have to hear that again."

Three more Cups within four years saw to that. •
— *Cam Cole*

4 The Great One always recognized a great script, and true to form, he saved his most prestigious scoring feat for the city where he came of age as a hockey player.

In one of those bittersweet moments that would tug Edmonton's heartstrings

each time Gretzky reaffirmed his greatness in his "second career" with the Kings, Wayne scored on Oilers goaltender Bill Ranford with 53 seconds left. His goal broke Gordie Howe's hallowed mark of 1,850 career points and tied the game, 3-3. Providing the evening's exclamation point, he scored the game winner in overtime.

"It was only fitting that it

Oct. 15, 1989: Replacing a legend with his 1,851st career point.

happened here," said Gretzky, who leapt from behind the net to score the record-breaker on the backhand. "I played a lot of years here and won four championships in this building."

The magnitude of Gretzky's assault on the Mount

Everest of NHL records? He scored his 1,851st point early in his 11th season, at age 28. Howe played 26 years, scoring his last point at age 51. •
— *Cam Cole*

5 The time: 14:47 of the second period.

The place: The Great Western Forum in Inglewood, Calif.

The moment: Wayne Gretzky, with a flick of his glittering, aluminum-shafted stick, breaks the mother of all NHL records — Gordie Howe's 801 career goals.

Accepting a cross-ice pass from Marty McSorley, Gretzky slipped his stick blade under the puck even before it kissed the ice and flipped it from the bottom of the left circle into the side of the net unguarded by Vancouver goalie Kirk McLean. Instantaneously, The Great One became The Greatest One.

As Gretzky leaped and raised his arms in exultation, "802" flashed on the scoreboard's jumbo screens, a red carpet was rolled to center ice and a swarm of photographers, their strobes crackling and flashes popping,

snapped enough pictures to fill several albums.

Canucks goalie McLean, who had jokingly contemplated hurling the historic puck into the stands before a Kings player could retrieve it, leaned against the goal and watched the celebration.

The game was suspended for 15 minutes for a ceremony that included NHL commissioner Gary Bettman; Gretzky's wife, Janet; his parents, Walter and Phyllis; and Kings owner Bruce McNall.

"It's a thrill to score one more goal than Gordie Howe, and I still can't believe I've done it," Gretzky said later. "I

March 23, 1994: Hockey's all-time goals king notches No. 802.

don't think words can describe the emotion that I felt at the time, the feeling I had and the gratitude I had for my teammates and, of course, for the fans. Nothing is the same as winning a championship, but I've got to tell you that this was pretty close." •
— *Rick Sadowski*

Cam Cole is a sports columnist for the Edmonton Journal.

Rick Sadowski covers the Los Angeles Kings for the Los Angeles Daily News.

chart
TOPPER

Wayne Gretzky ranks winning his first Stanley Cup title No. 1 on his list of career accomplishments

By Mike Pagel

Nothing tops the feeling of winning a Stanley Cup championship for the first time.

At least, not for Wayne Gretzky.

Of all his phenomenal accomplishments, Gretzky personally rates Edmonton's 1984 Stanley Cup championship as the greatest moment of an illustrious career that spans almost two decades. The 1984 title represents the first of four titles for Gretzky and the Oilers in a five-year stretch.

Prior to the 1995-96 season, Gretzky reflected on his 16 seasons in the NHL and created a list of his top 10 greatest moments. The list became the focus for his latest video, *Wayne Gretzky's All-Star Hockey, Vol. 2 — Drills*, which was released in late 1995.

Each of Gretzky's top 10 moments features video highlights of the accomplishment, with narration from The Great One himself.

The memories Gretzky shares of his No. 1 moment remain as strong today as they were during the spring of '84, when the Oilers celebrated their first Stanley Cup title.

"When we won, I can remember the emotional breakdown was so strong," he says in the video. "And for me, I was fortunate that I was the captain and I was the guy who [was presented with] the Stanley Cup. And if

you've ever lifted it, it's pretty heavy. For that moment you can lift it up with one hand; you're on such a high.

"I remember the last few seconds of the game, just thinking, 'I've waited my whole life for this. This is going to be the most enjoyable moment of my life.'

"And those five seconds summed up a life of commitment and hard work, not only for me but for every player on our hockey team to finally get a chance to lift the Stanley Cup."

Three years prior to the Oilers' 1983-84 title season, Gretzky experienced another thrilling postseason moment as Edmonton shocked the hallowed Montreal Canadiens with a first-round sweep.

After Edmonton stole two games from the Canadiens in Montreal, Oilers' fans saluted their team when it returned to Edmonton.

"This particular night when we came out onto the ice, I don't think any of us had ever heard that kind of ovation before," Gretzky says. "I can remember the scene in the locker room. You don't even realize what you've accomplished because we were so young and we probably were as shocked or more shocked than anybody.

"That kind of set the tone of what was going to be expected from our team [in the 1980s]."

After Gretzky created the handwritten list, The Great One signed it and sent it to Michael T. Merhab, head of collectibles and media projects for the National Hockey League Players' Association.

Gretzky's autograph at the bottom of the list is of particular interest because he included his middle initial "D." He usually doesn't include the initial unless he's signing something official such as a legal document.

As Gretzky ventures into the last few seasons of his career, one could only wonder what new accomplishments will find a position in his ultimate top 10 list.

Odds are good that another Stanley Cup title will rank among his greatest moments. After all, he is the ultimate team player. Stay tuned. •

Mike Pagel is an assistant editor at Beckett Publications.

A Season For the Ages

By scoring 92 goals and 212 points, Wayne Gretzky turned the 1981-82 season into his personal work of art

By Jim Matheson

Gretzky won over Esposito's Hart in 1981-82.

The season Wayne Gretzky skated into the Twilight Zone for the first time, passing 200 points, somebody asked Bobby Orr to rate No. 99.

"On a scale of one to 10, what is he?" a fellow asked.

"He's about a 60," replied Orr.

Nobody laughed. Gretzky's memorable '81-82 season was the first time in NHL history that a player scored 200 points and it was the closest anyone's gotten to 100 goals.

At the heart of this season to remember was the greatest individual run in the game's history.

In one unbelievable stretch in late December of 1981, Gretzky scored 15 goals in five games. Nine goals were tallied in the last two, including five on a wonderful Dec. 30 night against Philadelphia.

On that night, Wayne hit the 50-goal milestone in the Oilers' 39th game (another first). He finished the season with 92 goals, and actually could have had more.

"I must have missed 25 breakaways," Gretzky admits.

On March 25, 1982, the night he reached the 200-point plateau against, of all teams, Calgary (Edmonton's heated rivals), Gretzky tallied four points. For the record, it was the third consecutive season that he scored four points on March 25. And you thought Gretzky didn't do things by device.

"Two hundred points? That's like hitting 80 home runs in a season or rushing for 3,000 yards in one year," said Edmonton assistant coach Billy Harris.

The Calgary fans started the night by booing No. 99 as the Battle of Alberta took shape. By night's end, they were giving him standing ovations.

"Some guy came up to me and asked me to autograph a $50 bill. I never thought I'd see that day," says Wayne's dad, Walter, who'd flown to Calgary with his wife, Phyllis for the game. "Wayne phoned before the game and said get on a plane. Like it never crossed his mind, he wouldn't get the 200 with us there."

Everything about that season worked out perfectly for Gretzky. After a mere mortal start to the season — seven points in five games — The Great One began to roll. The wasteland of would-be defenders left in his wake wasn't pretty:

• Defenders held Gretzky scoreless in just eight of 80 games.

• In 61 of those games, he scored at least two points.

• He scored at least one goal in 55 games, with 10 hat-tricks.

• Twelve times he scored five points.

• He also registered six- and seven-point outings in December, the same month he rang up a remarkable 44 points in 14 games.

"Trying to stop Wayne is like throwing a blanket over a ghost," said Kings head coach Parker MacDonald.

On the night he became the fastest 50-goal scorer of all-time, the usually humble Gretzky fessed up.

"[That was] probably the greatest game I ever played," he said.

Flyers head coach Pat Quinn wasn't about to argue.

"Any superlatives I might offer would be inadequate," Quinn said.

Gretzky scored his 46th goal on a tap-in past goalie Pete Peeters from the lip of the crease. He ripped a 35-footer for his 47th, a 25-footer for his 48th and a 30-footer for No. 49. Then, with Peeters off the ice in favor of a sixth attacker, Gretzky closed the festivities with an empty-netter for the historic No. 50.

"Hey I wasn't going to be in the

The Great One was at his best Dec. 30, 1981, when he became the fastest player to reach 50 goals in a season.

Gretzky's teammates swarmed the superstar in celebration after he broke the 200-point barrier on March 25, 1982.

record books," shrugged Peeters, forever grateful he was sitting out of harm's way on the bench when No. 99 slid a 30-footer into the unguarded net with five seconds left.

Bobby Clarke, still playing and still a force, sat in the Flyers' locker room after it was over and his eyes said it all. They rolled to the heavens with a look of amazement.

"This was absolutely crazy," the Hall of Famer said. "At least with Bobby Orr you'd see him wind up in his own end and you could try to set up some kind of defense to stop him. Gretzky comes out of nowhere. It's scary."

Even Gretzky's teammates, accustomed to such performances, were amazed at the feat.

"How was this supposed to happen?" said Oilers defenseman Paul Coffey. "Wayne had nine goals the last two games [four against Los Angeles Dec. 27]. He wanted to do it before the 40th game. You could have bet $1 million against him doing it, but I wasn't going to be the one [to make the bet]."

Remarkably, Gretzky remained patient and never forced shots during his five-game, 15-goal barrage. He took just 32 shots.

He also didn't forget his linemates, finding Dave Lumley in Colorado to run Lumley's scoring streak to 12 games.

"I had to bust my butt to get into the play and Wayne looked me square in the eye as if to say 'here it is,' " Lumley says, recalling the memory. "When I got to 10 straight games, I was tied with Bobby Hull, Mike Bossy and Andy Bathgate. They've watched me play. I'm sure they're all saying 'how in the hell can Dave Lumley score in all those games?'

Well, he had Gretzky passing him the puck. That's how."

Obviously, Gretzky had his mind on scoring, as well. He broke the NHL record for goals in a season (Phil Esposito — 76) with three on a blustery February night in Buffalo, with Espo tagging along for moral support.

"My wife told me when we went out for dinner to celebrate my birthday that Wayne would do it the next day. I remember saying 'OK, let's have a few more [drinks],' " laughed Espo.

"Seven years before, my dad told me a boy in the Soo [Sault Ste. Marie, Ont.] only 14 years old was going to break all my records," Espo recalls.

Gretzky took 284 shots to reach the 76-goal mark. Esposito needed 550 shots to hit 76.

A six-game "slump" in March cost Wayne a chance at 100 goals. Still, the 212-point, 92-goal season isn't too shabby.

"I guess the best way to describe my feelings," said Gretzky, "is to say I feel exactly like the guy who got 100 points for the first time. Who was that anyway?"

His name was Esposito, the name you erased from the record books.   •

Jim Matheson has covered the Oilers for The Edmonton Journal *since the team entered the NHL in 1979.*

Wayne Gretzky's pride for his native land never was more apparent or inspiring than during the compelling 1987 Canada Cup

By Scott Morrison

Oh, CAN'ADA!

They're a series of magical images that refuse to quit the collective memory of both a hockey-mad country and the player who helped create them.

"As far as I'm concerned," begins Wayne Gretzky, "I don't think you will ever see better hockey than what was played in that series. For me, it was probably the best hockey I've ever played."

It was the 1987 Canada Cup, a six-nation tournament that brought together the greatest hockey players in the world. And for Gretzky, the competition was more than a mere footnote to his career. It was a highlight.

He was tired that summer, after another grueling run through the playoffs. Gretzky and the Edmonton Oilers had won their third Stanley Cup in four years. He already had participated in one Canada Cup, so it would have been understandable if he had begged off this one. When the call came to serve his country, he paused, but Gretzky's answer never really was in doubt.

"I remember," says Alan Eagleson, organizer and founder of the Canada Cup, "there were times when he was really beat, but I knew he would say yes. That's just the kind of guy he is."

Patriotic and proud. That's Gretzky. He may have moved to the United States but he never has forgotten his small-town Canada roots. Wearing the red maple leaf and representing his country in international competition always has meant something special to him, which is why he remains so keen about one day playing in the Olympics. But he found another reason to say yes in 1987. The best players in the world would be present. He saw a challenge at hand, a bell to answer.

As usual, when the dust settled, Gretzky stood as the best of the best.

In a career that's seen Wayne win four Stanley Cups, 10 scoring championships, nine Most Valuable Player awards and establish himself as hockey's most prolific scorer ever, the Canada Cup represents

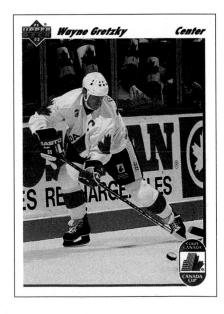

The card back of Wayne's 1991-92 Upper Deck #13 recounts his play during four tournaments.

something unique to Gretzky.

He has played in four of them: his first in 1981, his last in 1991. He led the tournament in scoring with a dozen points in 1981, but Canada lost in the final to Russia. In 1984, he again led in scoring with 12 points, and the Canadians won. In 1991, another victorious year for Canada, he totaled a dozen points in seven games before suffering a back injury in the playoff round.

The 1987 tournament, though, provided the collection of magical moments to an already remarkable career. Gretzky posted an incredible 21 points in nine games. But it was his ability to raise his game to another level and carry a team to glory that made the event truly memorable.

His virtuoso performance heightened the already immense regard for his talents and reverence in which he's held in Canada. A national treasure by that time, Wayne became an even more heroic figure for leading Canada to victory over the Soviet Union. Canada's triumph came at a time when the Big Red Machine still was a hated foe, and it occurred in a final series that rivaled the dramatics and entertainment value of the epochal 1972 Canada-Russia series.

"It's just phenomenal," said Team Canada coach Mike Keenan afterward, "what Wayne was able to do."

The Soviets won the series opener in overtime. In the second game, the Canadians opened a 3-1 lead, but required a double-overtime goal from Mario Lemieux for victory. Some called that second game the greatest game ever played.

In the deciding contest, Canada fell behind 3-0 and 4-2, rallied to take a 5-4 lead, then lost it. But with just 1:26 remaining in the game, Gretzky carried the puck up the ice, fed Lemieux a perfect pass, and Mario converted it into the winning goal.

Lemieux, who often played on the right wing on Gretzky's line, admitted to playing his best hockey ever during the tournament. Keenan knew why: Gretzky's play inspired Lemieux, challenging him to reach a higher level of excellence. Fittingly, Gretzky delivered the pass to Lemieux for the clincher.

Gretzky derived satisfaction not only from winning, but also from playing, arguably, the best hockey of his career. Any doubt he was the world's greatest player was obliterated during that series.

"It's hard to compare the feeling of winning the first Stanley Cup, or any of them, with the Canada Cup," Gretzky says. "It's very different. In the Canada Cup, you're together as a team for a month. It's a very intense period. But it's always a great honor to represent your country, and it's a great thrill when you win, especially when you beat the best teams in the world.

"It's a different challenge, and it's something I've always enjoyed doing," Wayne adds. "In that tournament, the hockey was great. Like I said, it was probably the best I've ever played."

Keenan remembers watching Gretzky one day before practice. Bearing the brunt of the media and fan attention, Gretzky appeared weary. But his demeanor changed the instant he stepped on the ice.

"It was like, at long last, he was in the one place where he felt the most comfortable," Keenan says. "It was the one place where he was at peace, where he could do what he wanted, and he could have fun."

On the ice is where Gretzky is at his best. In the 1987 Canada Cup, he never was better. •

Scott Morrison is a columnist for the Toronto Sun.

Gretzky's example in the brilliantly competitive 1987 Canada Cup inspired a magnificent performance from linemate Mario Lemieux.

BRUCE BENNETT / B. BENNETT STUDIOS

The Christmas in question was around 1967. Even Wayne Gretzky can't recall the exact year anymore. That December, all he wanted for Christmas was a Detroit Red Wings' sweater. But not just any sweater. A sweater with No. 9 on the back.

Gordie Howe's number.

Gordie Howe's sweater.

"I was just 5 or 6 years old," Gretzky recalls. "My best-ever Christmas. I don't think I opened another present. The sweater made my life. I wore it everywhere for a whole year."

Growing up in Brantford, Ontario, about 300 miles from Detroit, Wayne idolized Howe, the brawny winger who eventually became the NHL's all-time goal scorer.

Some years after that momentous Christmas, Gretzky met Howe for the first time. That came the year he turned 11. A hockey phenomenon, Gretzky scored goals at such an incredible rate that *Hockey Night in Canada* deemed him worthy of a feature. Howe, one of the most respected players in the NHL, attended a sports banquet in Brantford also attended by Gretzky. They posed for the now-famous picture — Howe with a stick wrapped around Gretzky's neck, as

if he were hooking him to the ice on a breakaway.

Since that inaugural meeting, their paths have crossed frequently, and their destinies have been forever linked. But these players who eventually arrived at the same, rarified destination — the 800-goal plateau — exhibited widely differing styles getting there.

Pound for pound, Howe arguably was the NHL's toughest player ever. He was legendary for going into corners

Foreve Lin

By Eric Duhatschek

Wayne Gretzky grew up idolizing hockey legend Gordie Howe. Their relationship has witnessed few idle moments ever since.

Linemates in the 1979 WHA All-Star Game, Gordie and Gretzky first crossed paths at a sports banquet in Brantford (opposite page).

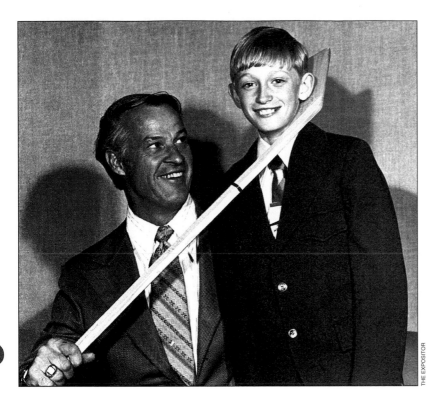

THE EXPOSITOR

ked

with his elbows up. If you dared to body-check him on a shift, he would note your number and exact his pound of flesh, likely on that shift.

By contrast, Gretzky tips the scales at a modest 180 pounds. His game revolves around an elusive quickness that keeps him from being checked into oblivion by the NHL's heavyweights.

"There have been times when I've said, 'Boy, I wish I was the size of Mark Messier. I'd crack a few guys,' " Gretzky says. "Or 'I wish I had Gordie Howe's strength. I'd do a few of the things that his reputation said he did during the years.' No, I really always did the best with what I have."

Apart from their prolific scoring

achievements, the only other similarity between the two legends is their respective longevity. Howe played into his 50s, eventually suiting up with his sons, Mark and Marty. Gretzky, entering his 18th pro season, will not be skating when or if son Ty ever turns pro. The changing economic climate suggests fewer stars will grind it out into their mid-30s.

Gretzky's initial on-ice encounter with his idol occurred in 1979, during Wayne's first pro season. Gretzky's second game for the Indianapolis Racers of the WHA was against Howe's New England Whalers. Howe gave Gretzky the wink and the "hi" sign in warm-ups, the way two old friends do.

"I was pretty awestruck and pretty excited," Gretzky recalls. "He was winking at me in warm-ups and tapped me in the shin pads. When I got on the ice about the third shift into the game, he was going down one wing, and I lifted his stick and took the puck and started going back the other way.

"All of a sudden, I felt this crack on my thumb. He took one hand, as he always did, and flicked his wrist and hit me on the thumb. I dropped my stick. He got the puck back and said, 'Don't ever embarrass me on the ice again.' "

They next met on-ice in the 1979 WHA All-Star Game in Edmonton. Howe played in All-Star games in five decades — from the 1940s to the '80s, — but this was Gretzky's first.

"Here I was, 17 years old, sitting beside Gordie Howe in the dressing room," Gretzky remembers. "He tells me, 'Just go to the front of the net' and he'll get me the puck. We scored nine seconds into the game. I remember coming back to our bench and shaking my head."

As Gretzky approached Howe's all-time NHL goals scoring record in 1994, the Hall of Famer did not follow Wayne around from game to game and arena to arena. He'd done that once already, when Gretzky surpassed his NHL points-scoring record in 1989. Howe begged off this time because of a series of previous commitments.

Howe, however, did cross paths with Gretzky at the 1994 NHL All-Star Game. Naturally, the two again fielded questions about their history with each other.

"I liked Wayne right away," Howe said. "Why? He said Mr. and Mrs. a lot. He said please and thank you."

In that respect, Gretzky hasn't changed very much. Nor have Gretzky's feelings toward Howe changed since that memorable Christmas.

"They often tell you," Gretzky remarks, "when you meet your heroes and idols, you walk away saying, 'Well, they're not that nice, or just OK.' But Gordie, he was bigger and better than I ever imagined."   •

Eric Duhatschek covers hockey for the Calgary Herald.

Gallery of Gretzky

Like Wayne Gretzky's career,
the following artistic pieces exhibit a
colorful brilliance all their own

Opie Otterstad • *Acrylic*

Amy Chenier • *Acrylic*

Andy Yelenak • *Watercolor*

Opie Otterstad • *Acrylic*

Dan Stromme • *Watercolor*

Rob MacDougal • *Watercolor*

ELUSIVE TARGET

Wayne Gretzky's cunning hockey sense and evasive nature invariably foil every

attempt to contain him

By Lance Hornby

Perhaps the next time great minds meet to discuss ozone depletion, colonizing Mars or curing the common cold, they'll have a few minutes for an old hockey conundrum.

Namely, how in heaven's name do you stop Wayne Gretzky?

It certainly has baffled the hockey sphere, those on the ice and behind the bench, causing mass insomnia, usually heightened during the Stanley Cup playoffs.

Gretzky's numbers — 1,010 total goals, 2,095 assists and 3,100 points in his 18 WHA/NHL seasons — vividly confirm no one's come up with a solution.

As a left-side defense-man, Jamie Macoun has been caught in Gretzky's headlights countless times in the last 12 years.

"The question I'm most often asked is why don't we just hit him," says Macoun, who now plays for the Toronto Maple Leafs. "But it's not that simple.

"You can't hit him when he's eight feet away. If you do try, you know he's watching you, too, and he's got wingers and defensemen all over the place to pass to."

Having grown up playing with boys and men much older than himself, Gretzky long ago became adept at keeping his body limp, passing or shooting, then spinning away from hits.

When Macoun played for the Calgary Flames in '86, former coach Bob Johnson devised a seven-point plan to stop The Great One, then a member of the Edmonton Oilers.

Calgary won the Stanley Cup playoff series in seven games, but no one recalls the Gretzky coverage being the turning point. Wayne recorded 19 points in 10 playoff games that spring.

"Knowing how Badger Bob liked to prepare, there were probably seven more points on Gretzky we had to memorize by the end of the first period," chuckles Macoun. "But it's got to be a team effort against Wayne."

Sticking one pesky checker on Gretzky to hound him all over the ice has been the universal strategy. But unlike bulky Mario Lemieux, or contemporaries in other sports,

such as Emmitt Smith or Charles Barkley, Gretzky is more a submarine than a battleship.

His role in a goal simply might be one pass instead of an end-to-end rush. But chances are, he'll have come out of nowhere to make the delivery and disappear just as quickly.

When all else fails, grabbing a handful of jersey is the best strategy against Gretzky.

"There's the old cliche that you'll slow him down, but you'll never stop him," says Buffalo GM John Muckler, who worked with Gretzky in Edmonton.

As Gretzky neared his 30s, it was clear he derived more pleasure from setting up goals than from scoring. Many assists came on plays started behind the net, which came to be known as "Gretzky's office."

"Once he's there," says former NHL goalie Mike Liut, "your mind is on the guy he's going to pass to, but you can't take your eyes off Wayne."

So creative is Gretzky from his office, "He once flipped it from behind there,

Shadowing Gretzky often proved futile, but former teammate Esa Tikkanen enjoyed some success at the task.

"[Esa] Tikkanen knew [Gretzky] better than any checker. Tikkanen will yap at him all the time."
— Steve Kasper

off my neck, and in," marvels Liut.

As teams deployed extra manpower on him, Gretzky, ever the tactician, evolved from prolific scorer to selfless playmaker. Consequently, many teams tried to neutralize his wingers.

Invariably, however, Gretzky always has the team's best sidekicks on his line; speedy Jari Kurri and Mark Messier from his Edmonton days, Luc Robitaille in Los Angeles and Brett Hull or Shayne Corson in St. Louis.

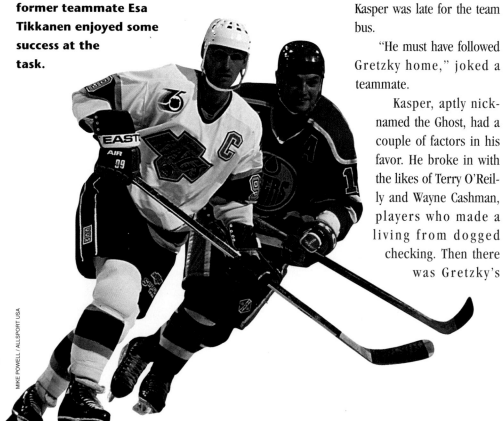

MIKE POWELL / ALLSPORT USA

There's not a place on the ice where Gretzky can't find them.

In 1994, despite a lack of offensive-minded partners on the Kings, Gretzky won his 10th league scoring title.

If you can't stop Gretzky, you can try to irritate him. The man Gretzky acknowledges as his greatest adversary is former Bruins center Steve Kasper. Kasper joined the league a year after Gretzky, and they had intense encounters through the 1988 Cup finals.

After one night of driving Gretzky crazy around Northlands Coliseum, which included following him to the door of the Edmonton bench, Kasper was late for the team bus.

"He must have followed Gretzky home," joked a teammate.

Kasper, aptly nicknamed the Ghost, had a couple of factors in his favor. He broke in with the likes of Terry O'Reilly and Wayne Cashman, players who made a living from dogged checking. Then there was Gretzky's

natural dislike for Boston Garden, a rink too small to wheel in.

"My goal was to stay between him and the net, make sure he had to go through me to play or pass," Kasper says. "Of course, I followed him as close as I could, not allowing him much time to think.

"In football, there's the bump-and-run, and I tried much the same thing to get him and slow him down before he got on stride."

Kasper emphasized he meant bumping, not mugging. If a Gretzky bodyguard such as Marty McSorley didn't avenge transgressions taken against No. 99, a Gretzky-led power play usually would make the offender pay.

Lastly, Kasper tried to approach Gretzky assignments as if he were preparing for the fourth-line center on an expansion team.

"You could psych yourself out worrying that he was Gretzky," Kasper says. "You felt like a fan watching him anyway."

In his autobiography, Gretzky acknowledged Kasper as the man he most hated to play against.

"When I got married," Gretzky writes, "I half expected to see Kasper standing at the alter in a tux."

Kasper thinks Esa Tikkanen, Gretzky's former Edmonton linemate, has been the most effective player he's seen on Wayne.

"Tikkanen knew him

Operating from his "office" behind the net, Wayne wreaks havoc with goalies' nerves and defensemen's patience.

better than any checker," Kasper laughs. "Tikkanen will yap at him all the time, where I was all business."

If a shadow became too much of a bother, Gretzky often would use reverse psychology and stand near an opposing defenseman. That almost would guarantee an odd-man rush for his team elsewhere on the ice.

Some clubs would pin a defenseman rather than a center or winger on Gretzky. The Flames achieved some success with Neil Sheehy.

To goaltenders, Gretzky

is like a Swiss Army knife, revealing a new blade, corkscrew or hidden tool every time.

"He's excellent at putting it where you aren't," says former goalie Rick Wamsley, now an instructor with the Leafs. "He owned me one night in St. Louis — four goals — and I think they were all in different spots. When he has the puck, we have to be aware of his wingers and options."

Adds Liut, who faced Gretzky for 12 seasons, "Wayne's two favorite plays are a) find the guy no one else but him can see, and b) lose himself in your end.

"It's like watching World Cup soccer: He's the guy always playing way wide. I'd deflect a puck to the corner

the way I've been taught and there's Wayne and I'm wondering, 'What's he doing there?'

"He's a genius," Liut concludes. "I'd see him come down the ice and immediately start thinking, 'What don't I see that Wayne's seeing right now?' "

Ironically, Gretzky's lone weakness lies in his performance on breakaways and penalty shots.

"Once he's [behind the net], your mind is on the guy he's going to pass to, but you can't take your eyes off Wayne."
— **Mike Liut**

"That might be because he rarely tries to beat a guy one-on-one," Wamsley observes. "He'd rather pass it, so he's not as used to being on breakaways."

But given his vast accomplishments, Gretzky can be forgiven the odd miss.

"No one in the world can do what he does," praises Stars winger Pat Verbeek. "He sees the whole ice where others see half.

"And your only hope in the world to stop him is that he comes to the rink and decides he doesn't want to play."

The common cold will be cured before that happens. •

Lance Hornby covers the NHL for the Toronto Sun.

Thanks For t

he Memories

Wayne Gretzky helps turn good players into stars, great players into superstars and even extends the careers of some thugs. Basically, he's the ultimate teammate.

By Damien Cox

During 18 years of cutting a brilliant swath of excellence through professional hockey, Wayne Gretzky has reached out to his many teammates.

In much the same way men once proudly laid claim to having skated on the same hockey club as Gordie Howe, Maurice "The Rocket" Richard or Bobby Orr, hundreds of players wear their moment in No. 99's spotlight as an athletic badge of honor.

From Mark Messier to Chris Pronger, from Jari Kurri to Andy Moog, from Mike Hudson to Paul Coffey, Gretzky has long been one of those players with the uncanny ability to leave lasting memories with those who have lined up alongside him.

Wherever Gretzky goes, he leaves goals, assists and memories. Unlike the

With L.A., he was a King. With Lemieux at the '87 Canada Cup, Gretzky was awesome.

goals and assists, the memories aren't always on target, however.

"I played with him one year. I figure I got him kick-started, and then he moved on from there," says Colin Campbell, a Gretzky teammate on the 1979-80 Edmonton Oilers team and now the head coach of the New York Rangers. "At least that's what I'll tell my grandchildren."

Dave Semenko was far from being a fabulously talented hockey player, but his pugilistic prowess won him the job with the Oilers as Gretzky's left winger for far more games than his basic hockey talent should have dictated.

"Talk about a prime ticket, I had one," wrote Semenko in his autobiography, *Looking Out For Number One*. "For nine years, I had the best seat in the house to watch him every time he played hockey. I was front row centre. People want to know how long it took Gretz to impress me? That's never been a tough one to answer. One shift."

The stories are as countless as

Wayne's career point total.

After years of being a star NHL blueliner who often opposed Gretzky, Al MacInnis suddenly found himself with The Great One after Gretzky was traded to St. Louis in February of 1996. MacInnis suggested that Gretzky's presence provided an intimidation factor.

"Let's face it," MacInnis says. "There are a lot of guys probably nervous to have a Wayne Gretzky in the dressing room."

Teammate Geoff Courtnall said the reaction of him and his teammates to the NHL's all-time scoring leader was demonstrated when the Blues boarded an early morning flight to meet Gretzky in Vancouver after the trade.

"It was the first time I'd seen bright eyes and players ready to go for a 7 o'clock flight," Courtnall says.

Todd Gill considered himself a run-of-the-mill defenseman with the Toronto Maple Leafs until Gretzky suddenly called him in the fall of 1994 and invited him on an NHL labor strife-

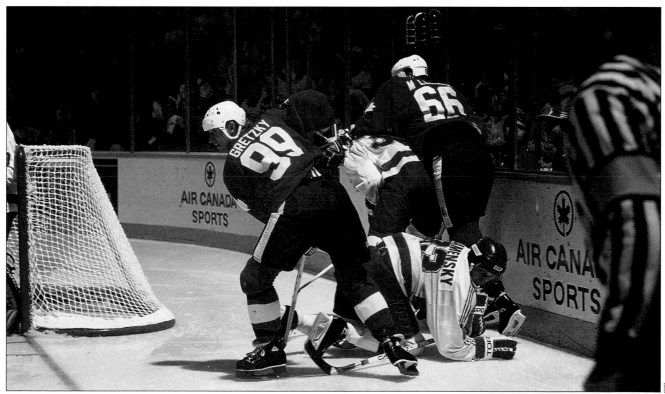

B. BENNETT / BBS

Many teammates helped Wayne
reach his milestone, but Jari
Kurri helped him celebrate it.

inspired tour of Europe.

Grant Fuhr, a future Hall of Fame goaltender, has played with Gretzky through many of the twists and turns of his career. Fuhr has played with Gretzky in Edmonton, Los Angeles and St. Louis, on Canada Cup teams and in world championships. When Gretzky was organizing his European tour, Fuhr was his first and only choice for goal.

"The biggest thing playing with Gretz is that he's a lot of fun to play with and he doesn't hold himself in a different light above everyone else. He likes to enjoy the game," Fuhr says. "He just makes everybody feel part of the team. He definitely makes everyone a better player. Even goalies. Everyone sees the level he plays at, and tries to get to that level."

The fact that he makes others better has been evident ever since Gretzky hit the NHL. During his first seasons in the league, he was paired with a couple of young wingers named Brett Callighen and B.J. MacDonald.

Callighen scored 48 goals in two seasons, and MacDonald potted 46 goals in the 1979-80 season alone.

After being separated from Gretzky neither player came close to that quality of hockey again.

At another level entirely was Gretzky's collaboration with Mario Lemieux at the 1987 Canada Cup, an international tournament now known as the World Cup of Hockey. Up until that point in his career, Lemieux had hit the 100-point level in each of his first three NHL seasons, but was viewed as a brooding, and sometimes lazy, super-talent.

At the '87 gathering, Lemieux elevated his game while skating on a line with Gretzky, scoring 11 goals in nine games against the toughest opposition on the planet. Super Mario capped off his run by winning the hearts of his country with the decisive, tournament-clinching goal against the Soviet Union off a Gretzky assist.

The next season, Lemieux won the first of his five NHL scoring titles, and many observers credited Gretzky with showing the stoic young French-Canadian star the way.

At the '91 Canada Cup, Gretzky again showed the way, this time for a phenom named Eric Lindros.

Lindros wasn't as dominant as Lemieux with three goals in eight games, but at least he began to see how the biggest names in hockey handle themselves on the ice.

"It was a lot of fun to see him and all the best players in the game just having fun playing," Lindros recalls.

Gretzky's genius, of course, lies in his ability to work with others. As a playmaker by trade — toss out his 92-goal season and his NHL-record 837 career scores for a moment — he always has shone brightest when engineering the successes of others.

In his first NHL season, he led the league with 86 assists, and quickly became known as a player who saw the ice better than anyone, and an athlete who could anticipate where the puck and the play was going before the actual moment materialized.

To possess that quality, and then use it to pass off to the likes of Kurri or Messier for a goal, requires an unselfish attitude. The result is a record 1,771 career assists for The Great One.

Some credit for that can be traced to his boyhood days when his father, Walter, on the family's outdoor rink, taught him that a pass was as good as a shot, and that the love of the game must always stand above everything else.

His reward has been wealth, nine Hart trophies as the NHL's Most Valuable Player, nine first team All-Star Game appearances and more than 100 points in 15 of his 17 seasons. The reward for his teammates has been four Stanley Cups and the fond memories of skating with one of the greatest ever to lace 'em up. •

Damien Cox covers the NHL for the Toronto Daily Star.

Jari Kurri assisted on 194 (24 percent) of Wayne's goals. Next closest is Paul Coffey with 116. In all, 102 players, including seven goalies, assisted on Wayne's 803 goals, from Mike Allison to Alexei Zhitnik.

LAST CALL

Gretzky scored six goals in games with one second on the clock.

JUMP START

Gretzky scored his quickest goal in a game eight seconds into the Dec. 14, 1983, match against Glen Hanlon and the New York Rangers.

TARGET PRACTICE

Wayne beat Richard Brodeur and Mike Liut 29 times each. All together, he victimized 139 goalkeepers, from Hardy Astrom to Wendel Young.

FAST DASH

Speed isn't one of Wayne's noted assets, but in reaching two scoring milestones, he's a relative sprinter compared to his closest pursuers.

500 GOALS
Wayne Gretzky
575 games
Mike Bossy
647 games
Phil Esposito
803 games
Jari Kurri
833 games
Bobby Hull
861 games

1,000 POINTS
Wayne Gretzky
424 games
Mario Lemieux
513 games
Mike Bossy
656 games
Peter Stastny
682 games
Jari Kurri
716 games

803...a

No one in NHL history has put the biscuit in the basket more than T
through the 1993-94 season — the season he eclipsed Gordie How

MILESTONE GOALS

No. 1: Oct. 14, 1979 vs. Vancouver and goalie Glen Hanlon at 18:51 of the third period, gaining a 4-4 tie for the Oilers.

No. 100: March 7, 1981 vs. Philadelphia (empty net)

No. 200: Oct. 9, 1982 vs. Vancouver (Richard Brodeur)

No. 300: Dec. 13, 1983 vs. N.Y. Islanders (Bill Smith)

No. 400: Jan. 13, 1985 vs. Buffalo (Tom Barrasso)

No. 500: Nov. 22, 1986 vs. Vancouver (empty net)

No. 600: Nov. 23, 1988 vs. Detroit (Greg Stefan)

No. 700: Jan. 3, 1991 vs. N.Y. Islanders (Glenn Healy)

No. 800: March 20, 1994 vs. San Jose (Arturs Irbe)

803 BREAKDOWN

442 Home

361 Away

72 First Goals

123 Final Goals

78 Game-Winning Goals

21 Game-Tying Goals

72 Shorthanded Goals

180 Power-Play Goals

46 Empty-Net Goals

1 Penalty Shot (Jan. 19, 1983 vs. Vancouver)

FAVORITE FOES

Winnipeg 76 goals
Calgary 67 goals
Vancouver 67 goals
Los Angeles 58 goals
Toronto 48 goals

ONCE IS NEVER ENOUGH

136 two-goal games
30 three-goal games
13 four-goal games
4 five-goal games

CELEBRATION SCORES

Gretzky has scored nine goals on Jan. 26., his birthday.

FAST TIMES

Gretzky scored a goal in the first minute of seven different games.

reat One. Here's a detailed look at the 803 goals he scored
cord to become the game's all-time goal leader.

G his GREA

Wayne says he's yet to achieve it. The example his father, Walter, established is a tough act to follow.

By Lance Hornby

He passed Howe, eclipsed Orr, and a few times, raised Stanley.

But the most difficult challenge facing Wayne Gretzky remains — being as good a father to his kids as his dad was to him.

Walter Gretzky has become famous in his own right for his storied relationship with his son and his homespun philosophy on the game, which Wayne's carried with him through a glorious National Hockey League career.

Say what you will about the lack of truth in advertising, but Walter's bit in a soft drink commercial with Wayne a few years ago came straight from the heart. The ad focused on a hockey school Wayne was running.

"All the kids and their dads meet at the end and there's Walter, waiting with a drink for Wayne," remembers Michael Barnett, Gretzky's agent and close friend. "Wayne says 'Thanks, Dad' and they walk out together. That really captures the essence of their relationship.

"They have such a profound friendship," Barnett adds. "Unnecessary words have never cluttered their relationship."

Wayne employs other means to display his affection for his father. A

Whether at home or at the rink, the Gretzky clan (Wayne, Janet, sons Trevor and Ty, and daughter Paulina) does things together.

ROBERT BECK

TEST goal

PAUL KENNEDY / SPORTS ILLUSTRATED

huge mural of father and son occupies an outer wall of Wayne's Toronto restaurant.

When Wayne plays in big games — Cup finals, Canada Cups, All-Star games — Walter always is there, the ever-dedicated hockey father, a scene many Canadians identify with. And he isn't afraid to critique Wayne after any of them, just as if they'd come off the backyard rink in Brantford, Ontario.

The bond began when 2-year-old Wayne toddled on skates on the Nith River near Brantford, survived a surreal celebrity career that began at age 10, strengthened during the golden '80s and matured during Walter's near death and brave recovery from a ruptured brain aneurysm.

"I was very fortunate," Wayne says, "to have the best teacher anyone could have in fundamentals in hockey and fundamentals in life. He doesn't have a college degree, but he's probably the smartest man I know."

And one of the most modest. Walter long has ducked the spotlight that natu-

rally follows the father of one of the greatest athletes of all time. He also has refused several gifts — including a new house and car — Wayne tried to pass his way. Walter prefers the quiet life with wife Phyllis in the same Brantford home where Wayne and his three brothers and sister were born.

Today, Wayne wants to give his three children, Paulina (7), Ty (5), and Trevor (4) as much as possible. The two boys immediately took a liking to hockey, roaring around Gretzky's Los

Proud parents Walter and Phyllis provided Wayne with lessons in life that he's surely passing on to his own family.

Angeles mansion at the crack of dawn in rollerblades or accompanying Dad to Kings practice to get some ice time.

"I don't want to push my sons," Wayne says. "I don't want to make them think that I'm making them do something. I tiptoe through it [hockey instruction]."

"When I do sit down with them," Wayne continues, "I try to talk about the basics: crossovers, two hands on the stick, keeping your head up — just stuff kids should know at a young age.

"[Ty] wants to play, loves to play. That's great. He has a lot of advantages if he wants to play. The downside of it is the amount of pressure he'll be under for the rest of his life if he wants to continue."

Ty will need his father's people skills, which go hand in hand with hockey. It's another trait Wayne learned from his Dad — and puts to good use in his role as the game's ambassador.

"What I taught Wayne is just part of living for anybody," Walter says. "He loved hockey, but he also knew he had to keep up his schooling.

"I always told him to give 110 percent out there, respect other people and treat them decently. He took it from there."

Wayne has tried to follow that path

Wayne's hockey career prevented him from spending a lot of time with brothers Keith and Brent (1992-93 Upper Deck #37) growing up, but he's always shared many special moments with Walter.

with his growing brood.

"I hope I'm raising my kids the same way that my parents raised our family," Wayne told the magazine *L.A. Sports Profiles*. "We [he and wife Janet] have no real formula of what is the right or wrong way for being a parent. One thing we all agree on is that you should teach your kids to respect people. Most of all, you should teach your kids that love is important, and you give them all the love and support you can."

As a 6-year-old, Wayne came home from a season-ending banquet in tears because he hadn't won a trophy. Walter urged him to keep practicing, and one day he'd have a house full of hardware,

a prophecy that obviously came true.

Walter built the famous backyard rink — the Wally Coliseum — and when his hockey-mad son ran out of friends to test his advanced skills against, Walter rounded up some older boys.

"Lots of kids as gifted as I was never had somebody like him to keep them on the right line," writes Wayne in his self-titled autobiography. "I don't know where I'd be without him, but I know it wouldn't be the NHL."

At 10, Wayne scored 378 goals in 69 games, earning national attention, but often he was vilified in Brantford by jealous and backbiting parents. Wayne actually would switch jackets with

KEITH, WAYNE & BRENT GRETZKY

BLOODLINES

teammate Greg Stefan, later an NHL goalie, just to avoid the harassment.

Though the callous remarks stung them as they sat in the stands, both Walter and Phyllis urged their son to let his actions do the talking.

Walter, whose own playing aspirations died when a bout of chicken pox cost him a tryout with the vaunted Toronto Marlborough juniors, insists there's nothing deep or mysterious about his own approach to the world.

Walter is the son of hardworking immigrants from Poland and Russia and remembers his own father as a man of few words. Given the chance to retire when Wayne first became a millionaire, Walter chose to go back to work for Bell Telephone. He figured it would look bad to his children to quit after years of telling them to work for their breaks.

Not one to play favorites, Walter and Phyllis invested as much time as possible in the careers of Wayne's brothers, Keith and Brent. The latter is a center in Toronto's farm system.

The Gretzky clan has accepted that Wayne's life now revolves around The Big Apple. But in the fall of 1991, Wayne couldn't be budged from his dad's side when a brain aneurysm threatened the elder Gretzky's life.

"I had about two weeks where they said he probably wouldn't live," Wayne recounted to the *Los Angeles Times*.

SPORTS ILLUSTRATED

"But I got lucky, and he came through. I saw my dad go from being my best friend to a guy who was strapped in a wheelchair."

At the time, Wayne was struggling with a career-threatening back injury and truly missed his father's counsel. But Walter is much improved these days, well enough to coach youth hockey in Brantford and co-star with Phyllis in a comical Canada Bell Telephone television commercial poking fun at Wayne's pregame long-distance call.

Amid their fishbowl life, Wayne and Janet, a well-known actress, have tried their best to act like a normal family.

"Wayne's feet are firmly on the ground," Barnett says. "You have to be close to him to understand the pressure he's subjected to. A simple transaction such as shopping or filling up the gas tank can be very difficult, and they have to go through that every day."

Regardless, Wayne will bust out of

Wayne and Janet's wedding received the royal treatment in Edmonton when they married in July 1988. Less than a month later, he was a King.

the fishbowl for his kids. During the Kings' run at the Stanley Cup during the 1992-93 season, Wayne refused to let someone else drive his daughter, Paulina, to preschool. No amount of inconvenience could replace that precious time.

And as was the case with the first Gretzky father-and-son commercial, Wayne and his son Ty recently shared the screen for an electronics company.

"Wayne has enormous respect for his parents and has passed that to his kids," Barnett says. "He's extremely grateful to his folks for the opportunity they've provided him with."

For Walter and Phyllis, seeing how Wayne turned out is thanks enough. •

Lance Hornby covers the NHL for the Toronto Sun.

Dadman's Dream

As an endorsement figure, Wayne Gretzky is the perfect spokesman — easily recognizable, a clean-cut family man, and dedicated to his product

By Kevin Allen

Wayne Gretzky scores as well on Madison Avenue as he does in any National Hockey League arena.

Experts believe the multi-million dollar salary he earned as an NHL player last season is less than the money he earns as a pitchman for a variety of international corporations. In advertising boardrooms on Madison Avenue and across America, The Great One plays in the same league with Michael Jordan, Ken Griffey Jr., Emmitt Smith and Charles Barkley.

"To me, Wayne is the best professional spokesman around," says Chris Jordan, Coca-Cola's director of consumer marketing. "In Canada, he's a national treasure. And in the United States, he is very well known."

When officials at Sharp — a company that makes a variety of consumer goods, including home entertainment products — sought a spokesman for their Viewcam commercials, they immediately thought of Gretzky.

"This was a unique product," says Dan Infanti, Sharp's vice president of corporate communication and marketing, about the company's high-tech video camera. "We wanted someone who stood out. And we wanted a family man, because the No. 1 purchaser of a Viewcam would be a young family."

As far as Sharp is concerned, the marriage of Gretzky and Viewcam is the best combination since coach Glen Sather put Gretzky and Jari Kurri together on the same line in Edmonton more than a decade ago. According to market research, recognition of the Viewcam went from zero to 40 percent immediately after Gretzky and his son Ty appeared in the family based commercials.

Gretzky's Q Rating — a barometer of his public appeal — is very high, say advertising executives. Both Infanti and Jordan believe Wayne's clean-cut image also makes him attractive to sponsors,

COURTESY OF COCA-COLA CANADA

who have become increasingly concerned about what their athletic spokesmen might do away from their arenas of competition. The biggest worry about Gretzky is whether he'll stop shaving for a few days.

"I wish everyone who is at the top of his profession treated people the way Wayne does," Infanti notes. "He is what his image is."

Gretzky's decisions on which products to endorse often prove just as important as the quality of the product.

Jim Easton, owner of the Easton sporting goods company, remembers the excitement in his office when Gretzky decided to use Easton's aluminum stick.

"A lot of dealers were sitting on the fence about aluminum," Easton recalls. "But after we signed Wayne, they started filling up their racks."

Few athletes can match Gretzky's unique position as a player synonymous with his sport. Michael Jordan owns the same recognition factor in basketball, as did Pele in soccer and Muhammad Ali in boxing.

Upper Deck was well aware of Wayne's stature when the card company signed Wayne to a seven-year contract in 1990. If image is important, then Upper

Deck could not afford to sign anyone else as its hockey spokesman.

"He's The Man," says Upper Deck's Paul Sackman, director of marketing services. "He's bigger than the game."

Gretzky's reputation for graciousness and remarkable sponsor loyalty entices many companies. For instance, before agreeing to represent Viewcam, he already was using one.

Coca-Cola's Jordan tells a story of how Gretzky showed up once at the Canada Cup training camp to find the arena was sponsored by Pepsi and had only Pepsi cups for the team's use. Because Gretzky and the Canadian team all were under the Coca-Cola sponsorship program, Wayne took matters into his own hands.

"Somehow he got a phone number for a local [Coca-Cola] dealer and asked him to bring over some cups," Jordan recalls.

While other athletes are interested only in making commercials and improving their own image, companies enjoy Gretzky's involvement in all levels.

When Coca-Cola decided to create a camp for kids, Gretzky provided ideas on how to organize the camp. And when Wayne chose his favorite players for '93-94 Upper Deck's Gretzky's Great Ones insert set, he insisted on writing the backs himself.

"He dictated them to [agent] Mike Barnett in the back of a limo," Sackman says. "And they were perfect."

Though he is careful not to let his off-ice activities interfere with his real job, Wayne did a series of promotional

The Gretzky viewers see in television commercials — such as this one with his father for Coca-Cola — is the real thing.

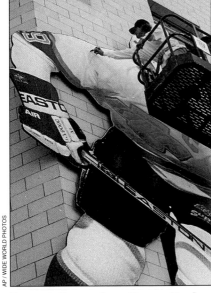

AP / WIDE WORLD PHOTOS

Companies such as Upper Deck Authenticated that employ Gretzky as a spokesman regard him as a larger-than-life figure.

commercials with comedian Denis Leary two years ago.

Always the center of attention, Gretzky this time played the straight man for Leary's humor. His ego never seems to come into play, despite his unofficial role as league promoter the last 17 seasons. Reporters encountering Wayne for the first time typically are impressed by his humility.

"He takes his role as league ambassador very seriously," Barnett points out.

Arthur Pincus, the NHL's vice president of public relations, and formerly an editor for the *Washington Post*, recalls a meeting his newspaper staff once had with NBA commissioner David Stern.

He asked Stern which player provided the most significant impact on the development of the NBA. He expected the answer to be either Larry Bird or Magic Johnson.

"But he said it was Julius Erving because he showed the other players how to act, how to be a player," Pincus recalls. "That's what Wayne Gretzky is to hockey. He's taught all the other players how to act." •

Kevin Allen is a sportswriter for USA Today.

Ever since Wayne emerged as a hockey superstar in the early '80s, he has made frequent visits to the front lines of celebrity. He's swapped uniforms with Jamie Farr on the set of *M*A*S*H*, appeared on *The Tonight Show with Jay Leno*, taken part in a photo shoot for *Sports Illustrated* with Magic Johnson and, along with the late John Candy and Kings owner Bruce McNall, once owned the Canadian Football League's Toronto Argonauts.

SNAP

WALTER IOOSS JR.

SHOTS

AP / WIDE WORLD PHOTOS

ON THE BALL

Growing up in Southern Ontario, Wayne also played lacrosse and baseball as well as hockey. In fact, the Toronto Blue Jays offered him a tryout the summer after his first NHL season (he declined). Although hockey remains Wayne's passion, he's kept a hand in other sports, whether through a game of touch football at a youth camp, tennis at a charity tournament, a relaxing round of golf or a ceremonial visit to a major league dugout with two of his three children.

STEVE BABINEAU

TIME PASSAGES

He joined the Edmonton Oilers in 1978 as a skinny 17-year-old. The most famous hockey player on the planet now is 35, a husband and a father of three. One way to mark Wayne Gretzky's career is charting his annexation of NHL records. Another way is noting the different "looks" he's sported throughout the years. But regardless of whether his locks are permed or shaggy, his face clean-shaven or goateed, Wayne's an appealing sight to collectors.

J. MICHAUD / B. BENNETT STUDIOS

B. BENNETT / B. BENNETT STUDIOS

SHARP SHOOTER

From any angle, Wayne Gretzky's shot remains one of the most lethal in the NHL. The pinpoint precision of one of Gretzky's bullets has left even the best goalies frozen in the crease.

Wayne Gretzky's profound effect as a collectible has left enduring skate marks on the hockey card hobby

hobby

KIN

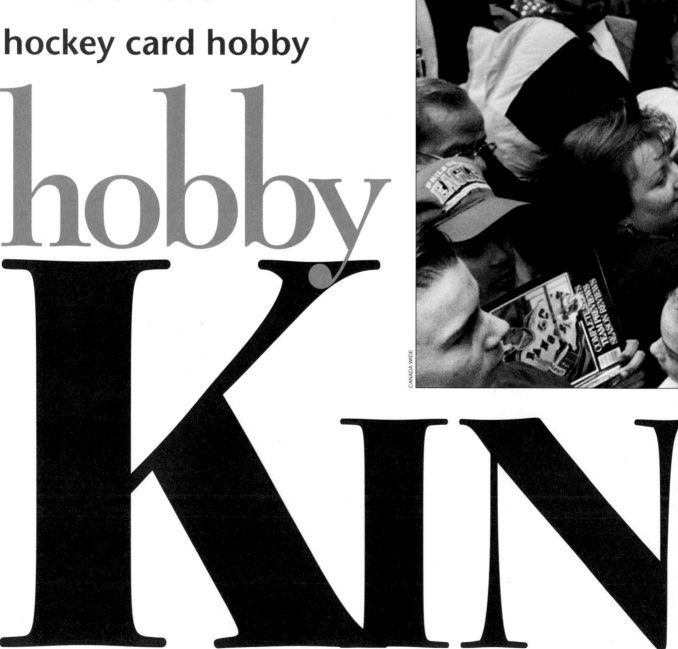

CANADA WIDE

By Tom Layberger

G

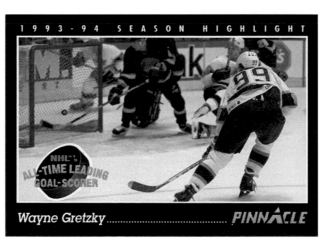

1993-94 SEASON HIGHLIGHT

NHL's ALL-TIME LEADING GOAL-SCORER

Wayne Gretzky .... PINNACLE

Signing wasn't always second nature to Wayne. "We were sitting in a restaurant and he grabbed a napkin," recalls Oilers public relations director Bill Tuele. "He wrote out his name five different ways, to try to get the right signature. I've still got the napkin."

As Wayne Gretzky put the finishing touches on his first NHL season in 1979-80, a campaign in which he scored 137 points and won the first of eight consecutive Hart trophies, many hockey observers believed this 19-year-old wunderkind could be the tonic the league needed to usher in a new era.

The NHL recently had concluded a successful battle with the World Hockey Association and absorbed four new teams and a plethora of new faces, including the teenage sensation from Brantford, Ontario. Fans that season welcomed new names in the standings and league leader categories.

For hockey card collectors, the '79-80 season achieved much the same effect, as it introduced cards of many players who never had appeared in a major set. One of the players was the fresh-faced Gretzky.

His initial cardboard likeness offered hockey collectors what his on-ice performance provided the league: a breath of fresh air. Gretzky ended the general boredom associated with 1970s hockey card issues and generated much of the impetus for the eventual modernization of hockey cards. But it would take some time before the value of his early cards became apparent.

Also issued during Gretzky's first NHL season was his 1979 Sportscaster #77-10. This odd-size issue is difficult to obtain and rivals his second-year O-Pee-Chee issue in value at about $150.

"The 1970s was a relatively flat time for hockey card collectors," says Gene Guarnere, a collector and dealer from West Chester, Pa. "When Gretzky entered the league, that was a time that marked expansion and a turnaround for the NHL. Gretzky became the league's first legitimate prospect since Guy Lafleur. That marked the beginning of hockey collectors taking interest in prospects or rookies."

Fifteen seasons and nearly 2,500 points later, Gretzky's Rookie Cards (1979-80 O-Pee-Chee and Topps #18) command $750 and $400, respectively. A collector needs to go back to the 1967-68 Topps #92 Bobby Orr to find a hockey card as valuable as Wayne's O-Pee-Chee RC. When assessing Gretzky's effect on the hobby, the central point is how his RCs heightened a general awareness of hockey cards.

As the cards matured in value, the impact was felt throughout the hobby. Collectors who didn't own a single hockey card inquired about Gretzky RCs. For many, a Gretzky RC would be their only hockey card. For others, interest in Gretzky stimulated interest in hockey cards in general.

For a number of reasons, but mainly because of a smaller print run, many collectors prefer the O-Pee-Chee issue to the Topps issue. Also, the paper quality of the Topps is substandard. Blue borders that are prone to chipping and poor methods of card cutting contribute to making this a difficult card to locate in ideal grades. Still, not too many $400 hockey cards exist.

Another landmark card in Gretzky collections is the 1988-89 Topps #120, depicting The Great One holding his new Los Angeles Kings sweater. The first card to reflect the historic transaction between the Oilers and Kings, it commands twice the value of its O-Pee-Chee counterpart.

"That's one card every Gretzky collector has to have," says Los Angeles collector and dealer Tom Hendriksen. "The card is easily one of the most popular among his mainstream issues."

Other challenging items of Gretzky in a Kings uniform

false START

Almost every collector knows that Wayne Gretzky's RC can be found in the 1979-80 OPC and Topps sets.

Many collectors, however, have inquired about another card, which pictures an adolescent Gretzky wearing the colors of his first professional team, the Indianapolis Racers. The card, which bears a slightly blurry photo and red borders, seems to predate the RC. So why isn't it considered the RC?

Without restrictions imposed through proper licensing, the card can be reprinted at any time. Its value, therefore, is no more than $1. Although it's unlikely to increase in value, it makes an interesting addition to any Gretzky collection. •

WAYNE GRETZKY
Indianapolis Racers - 1978

cardboard JEWELS

A list of Wayne Gretzky's 10 most valuable cards

1. 1995-96 Be A Player Die-Cut Signature #S97, $2,000: Although not as limited as originally announced (234 copies instead of 99), this remains an extremely desirable — and extremely tough — card to pull.

2. 1995-96 Finest gold Refractor #180, $1,250: According to the wrappers, fewer than 150 of these exist, making it Wayne's shortest- printed trading card. For hardcore collectors only.

3. 1994-95 Be A Player Signature #108, $1,200: The key card of the most popular hockey set of 1994-95. Limited to 300 copies and features a great shot of the Great One in NHLPA togs.

4. 1979-80 OPC #18, $850: The cornerstone of any serious Gretzky collection. Tough to find nicely centered with sharp edges.

5. 1995-96 Be A Player Signature #S97, $700: Conversely, this card is tougher to pull than announced (648 copies as opposed to 802). A more affordable option than No.1.

6. 1994-95 Pinnacle Artist's Proof #200, $500: It's just a bit of extra gold foil, but the long odds of finding one make this one of his most sought-after parallel cards.

7. 1979-80 Topps #18, $400: With sharper colors, cleaner edges and greater accessibility, this is the Gretzky RC of choice for those who demand Minty-Mint cards.

8. 1995-96 Pinnacle Artist's Proof #101, $400: More aesthetically pleasing than it's predecessor, this card also is a somewhat easier pull.

9. 1995-96 Summit Artist's Proof #24, $300: Obviously the matchup of the Great One with Pinnacle's high end Artist's Proof parallel concept has been enthusiastically received. The gold prism background really makes this one pop.

10. 1994-95 Finest Refractors #41, $300: The craze for Refractors instigated in other sports spilled readily into the hockey market. Even non-puckheads could be seen scouring for this card.

— Allan Muir

are postcard-size sheets produced by Upper Deck that were given to season ticket holders. Commanding at least $100 apiece, these sheets were limited to a print run of 7,000. A 1991-92 version commemorates the Kings' 25th anniversary, and the 1992-93 sheet serves as a holiday greeting card.

A variety of mainstream and peripheral card issues attracted collectors before Gretzky arrived in Southern California.

Red Rooster Food Stores of Alberta issued an Edmonton Oilers team set for the 1981-82 season that caused a mild controversy. The first printing featured four Gretzky cards picturing The Great One with long hair. The photos didn't meet with Wayne's approval and were destroyed in favor of the more common cards that show Wayne with much shorter hair. The nixed versions are so scarce it's not uncommon to see them fetch at least 20 times ($200) as much as the second versions.

In 1982, Ontario-based Neilson's Chocolates released a 50-card Gretzky set with cards inserted two per candy bar package. Extremely popular with collectors, the set was unique for featuring multiple cards of a player who'd been in the NHL just three years, demonstrating the impact Gretzky was beginning to exert on the hobby.

The set, which highlights Gretzky's childhood

Wayne's 1993-94 PowerPlay Point Leaders #3 leads the way in this 20-card set.

and his professional career, remains popular in part because of its affordability. Most single cards can be had for a five-dollar bill. The most valuable card in the set pictures Gretzky with boyhood hero Gordie Howe (#10) and commands $20.

Though there are many popular cards of Gretzky in an Oilers uniform, his trade to Los Angeles proved a boon to collectors. The trade coincided with the maturation of the hockey card industry.

Many consider the 1990-91 season the launching pad toward the new era in hockey cards, marking the first time O-Pee-Chee and Topps didn't serve the industry by themselves.

Pro Set, Score and Upper Deck offered collectors a greater sense of choice. Upper Deck helped ignite the new era by issuing a two-card promotional set at the 1990 National Sports Collectors Convention in Arlington, Texas. The set

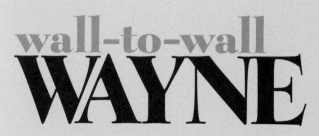

wall-to-wall WAYNE

Ever been shadowed by Wayne Gretzky for a full day? Considering the scope of Gretzky-related items produced throughout the years, it's possible to spend an entire day with The Great One.

Any superstar athlete likely will spawn countless collectibles. But an icon such as Wayne Gretzky? The only boundaries are the limitless imaginations of marketers. So prevalent is Wayne as a commercial entity, you could spend virtually every waking minute surrounded by Gretzky items.

Exaggeration? Hardly.

The characters in this day-in-the-life are fictional, but all the collectibles are real.

6:30 a.m. A Wayne Gretzky alarm clock rings at your bedside, signaling the start of a new day. Your eyes open to a Wayne Gretzky Titan sticks poster you received for making a purchase at Zellers department store on a trip to Canada. It hangs proudly with other Gretzky endorsement posters on your wall, which happens to be decorated with Gretzky wallpaper. Rolling out of bed, you fold your pajamas and place them under a set of Gretzky pillows, currently selling for about $25.

By Mike Hersh

7:15 a.m. Breakfast. What to have? What else? — Pro Stars cereal, featuring Gretzky on the box. Devouring the cereal, you leaf through the new Upper Deck Authenticated catalog, picturing Wayne and son Ty on the cover. This is the place for one-stop shoppers: signed and unsigned items such as oversized cards, hockey sticks, figurines and jerseys. Prices range from $29.95 for unsigned, oversized cards to $1,299 for the Gretzky collection (a signed jersey, puck, oversized card, heroes card and a personalized letter). Checking your Gretzky wristwatch, you realize it's time for work. So you throw your Gretzky Class Mate Calculator and Ruler calculator (distributed by Trans World Sales Inc.) into your briefcase.

8:30 a.m. Drats. En route to work, you accidently throw your 1983 Wayne Gretzky Edmonton Oilers dollar coin (worth $10-$15) into the toll basket.

9:10 a.m. You spend all morning at the office making calls on the Original Wayne Gretzky 99 Telephone, also distributed by Trans World Sales.

12:05 p.m. Lunchtime. Better yet, you have food from two different Aladdin Wayne Gretzky lunch boxes to choose from.

1:10 p.m. Now for some phone shopping. Hockey equipment dealer Milt Byron of Bargaintown, N.J., says game-used items have witnessed a boom in recent years. (A word of caution: Quite a few of Wayne's Kings jerseys are known to be fakes. Purchase jerseys from reputable dealers.) Titan and Easton sticks used by Gretzky are popular items, and they go for about $1,000-$1,500. The Titans are more prized by collectors because that's the model Gretzky used to set most of his NHL records. (He switched to Easton sticks beginning with the 1991-92 season.)

BRAD NEWTON

featured Gretzky and Montreal goaltender Patrick Roy.

Collectors clamored for The Great One promo and its innovative photography. Fueled by hype surrounding Gretzky, the price for the pair of cards hit upward of $100.

Gretzky's visibility within the hobby also soared as this release coincided with Upper Deck naming him a spokesperson for the company.

"Combined with the changes in the card, [Gretzky's] presence with the

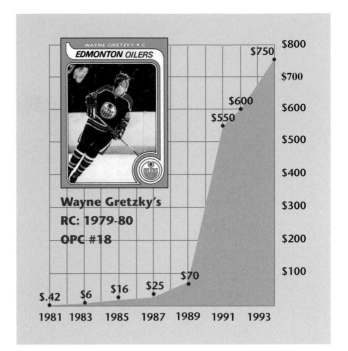

Wayne Gretzky's
RC: 1979-80
OPC #18

5:45 p.m. Home from work, you're horrified to find your son and his friends playing street hockey with your 1985 Titan Wayne Gretzky collectors series hockey stick, won through a contest at Zellers. Just 200 sticks were produced and signed by Gretzky. Worse, they're also using Gretzky commemorative pucks sold through his Toronto restaurant. One features his 802nd goal ($50), the other is an autographed photopuck depicting his 1,850th point ($75).

Meanwhile, your daughter and her friends have upstaged Ken and married Barbie to the Wayne Gretzky doll. Produced by Mattel, the Gretzky doll presently sells for $60-$80. At one point, you could buy a case of six dolls for $42.

Gretzky collectibles are almost as numerous as his goals.

She's also using the clothes that were sold separately from the doll. These items truly are scarce and rarely are seen on the market. The three different outfits include a jogging suit, tuxedo and an away uniform.

6:35 p.m. Now it's the Mrs. testing your blood pressure. She's serving dinner on your collection of Gartlan USA plates, one of which was signed by Gretzky and Gordie Howe ($225).

11:10 p.m. Before hitting the sack, you curl up with Wayne's autobiography, *Gretzky.* Drifting off to sleep, you dream of the collectibles still on your want list. But that's a story for another day. •

Mike Hersh is a freelance writer based in Cherry Hill, N.J.

Kings and the Kings' new colors opened arenas for marketing possibilities," says Frank Hurtado, owner of Y Not Cards in Chino Hills, Calif. "People who never collected suddenly were trying to get all of Gretzky's cards and became hooked on hockey cards in general."

Not long thereafter, card companies began using gold foil as a prominent component of their regular issues and insert sets. The first Gretzky gold card arrived in the 1992-93 Topps Gold set (#1). With inserts at one per pack, the set became hot, fueling rumors of short prints. The combination of Gretzky's appeal and speculation his issue (#1) was one of the short prints created a frenzy that sent the card to the $40 level.

Topps produced another parallel insert with the 1993-94 Stadium Club First

Day Issue. Certain to be popular on its own merits, the card received a boost when collectors discovered variations of his FDI. The Canadian version exists with the FDI imprint on either the top right or left. To complete the variations set, the American version has the imprint on the right side only. The diehard Gretzky fan will pay $200 apiece for these cards.

As evidenced by the abundance of key cards, Gretzky's impact on the hobby has been unmistakable and profound. From popular Rookie Cards to intriguing regional issues to cards that signal a new era to the search for variations, Gretzky and collectors of his likeness have charted a prosperous course for the hockey card hobby. •

Tom Layberger is a Price Guide analyst for Beckett Publications.

Wayne Gretzky
Comprehensive Card Checklist and Price Guide

☐ 1979 Sportscaster #77-10 $300
☐ 1979-80 O-Pee-Chee #18 $850
☐ 1979-80 Oilers Postcards #9 $50
☐ 1979-80 Topps #18 $400
☐ 1980-81 O-Pee-Chee #3 RB $35
☐ 1980-81 O-Pee-Chee #87 AS $50
☐ 1980-81 O-Pee-Chee #163 LL
  w/ Dionne and Lafleur $15
☐ 1980-81 O-Pee-Chee #182 TL $20
☐ 1980-81 O-Pee-Chee #250 $150
☐ 1980-81 O-Pee-Chee #162 LL
  w/Dionne, Lafleur $15
☐ 1980-81 O-Pee-Chee
  Super #7 $20
☐ 1980-81 Topps #3 RB $20
☐ 1980-81 Topps #87 AS $25
☐ 1980-81 Topps #162 LL w/
  Dionne and Lafleur $10
☐ 1980-81 Topps #163 LL w/
  Dionne and Lafleur $10
☐ 1980-81 Topps #182 TL $15
☐ 1980-81 Topps #250 $100
☐ 1981-82 O-Pee-Chee #106 $60
☐ 1981-82 O-Pee-Chee
  #125 SA $25
☐ 1981-82 O-Pee-Chee
  #126 TL $10
☐ 1981-82 O-Pee-Chee
  #383 LL $10
☐ 1981-82 O-Pee-Chee
  #384 LL $10
☐ 1981-82 O-Pee-Chee
  #392 RB $10
☐ 1981-82 O-Pee-Chee
  Stickers #209 $7.50
☐ 1981-82 O-Pee-Chee
  Stickers #252 $7.50
☐ 1981-82 O-Pee-Chee
  Stickers #264 $7.50
☐ 1981-82 Oilers
  Red Rooster #99 $10
☐ 1981-82 Oilers
  Red Rooster #99 $10
☐ 1981-82 Oilers
  Red Rooster #99 $10
☐ 1981-82 Oilers
  Red Rooster #99 $10
☐ 1981-82 Oilers
  West Edmonton Mall #3 $75
☐ 1981-82 Topps #16 $10
☐ 1981-82 Topps #52 $3
☐ 1982-83 McDonald's
  Stickers #20 AS $5
☐ 1982-83 McDonald's
  Stickers #22 $8
☐ 1982-83 Neilson's Gretzky Set
  50 cards $200

☐ 1982-83 O-Pee-Chee #1 HL $10
☐ 1982-83 O-Pee-Chee #99 TL $6
☐ 1982-83 O-Pee-Chee #106 $40
☐ 1982-83 O-Pee-Chee
  #107 IA $15
☐ 1982-83 O-Pee-Chee #235 LL $6
☐ 1982-83 O-Pee-Chee #237 LL
  w/ Michel Goulet $6
☐ 1982-83 O-Pee-Chee #240 LL $6
☐ 1982-83 O-Pee-Chee #242 LL $6
☐ 1982-83 O-Pee-Chee #243 LL $6
☐ 1982-83 O-Pee-Chee
  Stickers #97 $6
☐ 1982-83 O-Pee-Chee
  Stickers #98 $6
☐ 1982-83 O-Pee-Chee
  Stickers #162 AS Foil $8
☐ 1982-83 O-Pee-Chee
  Stickers #256 $4
☐ 1982-83 O-Pee-Chee
  Stickers #257 $4
☐ 1982-83 O-Pee-Chee
  Stickers #258 $4
☐ 1982-83 O-Pee-Chee
  Stickers #259 $4
☐ 1982-83 Oilers
  Red Rooster #99 $6

1986-87 Topps #3

☐ 1982-83 Oilers
  Red Rooster #99 $6
☐ 1982-83 Oilers
  Red Rooster #99 $6
☐ 1982-83 Oilers
  Red Rooster #99 $6
☐ 1982-83 Post Cereal #6
  Edmonton Oilers with 15
  other players $20

☐ 1983-84 Belleville Bulls #27 $35
☐ 1983-84 O-Pee-Chee #22 TL $6
☐ 1983-84 O-Pee-Chee #23 HL
  w/ Mark Messier $25
☐ 1983-84 O-Pee-Chee #29 $35
☐ 1983-84 O-Pee-Chee
  #203 AW $6
☐ 1983-84 O-Pee-Chee
  #204 AW $6
☐ 1983-84 O-Pee-Chee
  #212 RB $6
☐ 1983-84 O-Pee-Chee
  #215 LL $6
☐ 1983-84 O-Pee-Chee
  #216 LL $6
☐ 1983-84 O-Pee-Chee
  #217 LL $6
☐ 1983-84 O-Pee-Chee
  Stickers #7 $5
☐ 1983-84 O-Pee-Chee
  Stickers #89 $5
☐ 1983-84 O-Pee-Chee
  Stickers #90 $5
☐ 1983-84 O-Pee-Chee
  Stickers #161 AS $4
☐ 1983-84 O-Pee-Chee
  Stickers #301 $4
☐ 1983-84 O-Pee-Chee
  Stickers #307 $4
☐ 1983-84 O-Pee-Chee
  Stickers #325 FOIL $6
☐ 1983-84 O-Pee-Chee
  Stickers #326 FOIL $6
☐ 1983-84 Oilers Dollars
  #H14 $15
☐ 1983-84 Oilers
  McDonald's #21 $8
☐ 1983-84 Puffy Stickers #1
  w/Risebrough/Naslund/
  Derlago/Brodeur/Babych $15
☐ 1983-84 Vachon #26 $50
☐ 1984-85 7-Eleven Discs #16 $12
☐ 1984-85 7-Eleven Discs #NNO
  Large Size measures 4-1/2" $20
☐ 1984-85 O-Pee-Chee
  #208 AS $6
☐ 1984-85 O-Pee-Chee #243 $20
☐ 1984-85 O-Pee-Chee
  #357 TL $5
☐ 1984-85 O-Pee-Chee
  #373 AW $5
☐ 1984-85 O-Pee-Chee
  #374 AW $5
☐ 1984-85 O-Pee-Chee
  #380 LL $5
☐ 1984-85 O-Pee-Chee
  #381 LL $5

☐ 1984-85 O-Pee-Chee
  #382 LL $5
☐ 1984-85 O-Pee-Chee
  #383 LL $5
☐ 1984-85 O-Pee-Chee
  #388 RB $5
☐ 1984-85 O-Pee-Chee Stickers #63
  Foil w/ Michel Goulet (#64) $3
☐ 1984-85 O-Pee-Chee Stickers
  #138 FOIL $4
☐ 1984-85 O-Pee-Chee Stickers
  #226 w/ Tom Barasso (#227) $3
☐ 1984-85 O-Pee-Chee Stickers
  #229 w/ Tom Barasso (#228) $3
☐ 1984-85 O-Pee-Chee Stickers
  #255 $3.50
☐ 1984-85 O-Pee-Chee Stickers
  #256 $3.50
☐ 1984-85 Oilers McDonald's
  Album #11 $15
☐ 1984-85 Oilers
  Red Rooster #99 $5

1992-93 OPC #220

☐ 1984-85 Oilers
  Red Rooster #99 $5
☐ 1984-85 Oilers
  Red Rooster #99 $5
☐ 1984-85 Oilers
  Red Rooster #99 $5
☐ 1984-85 Oilers
  Team Issue #7 $10
☐ 1984-85 Topps #51 $8
☐ 1984-85 Topps #154 AS $2.50
☐ 1985 Islanders Islander News
  Trottier #21 w/ Brian Trottier $6
☐ 1985-86 O-Pee-Chee #120 $30
☐ 1985-86 O-Pee-Chee
  #257 LL $7
☐ 1985-86 O-Pee-Chee
  #258 LL $7
☐ 1985-86 O-Pee-Chee
  #259 LL $7
☐ 1985-86 O-Pee-Chee Box
  Bottoms #G $20
☐ 1985-86 O-Pee-Chee
  Stickers #5 $3.50
☐ 1985-86 O-Pee-Chee Stickers #54
  Foil w/ Vezina Trophy (197) $2.50
☐ 1985-86 O-Pee-Chee Stickers
  #120 Foil $4
☐ 1985-86 O-Pee-Chee Stickers
  #198 w/ Dennis Potvin (70) $3
☐ 1985-86 O-Pee-Chee Stickers
  #202 w/ Greg Gilbert (75) $3

❏ 1985-86 O-Pee-Chee Stickers
  #222 $3.50
❏ 1985-86 Oilers McDonald's
  Album #20 $12
❏ 1985-86 Oilers
  Red Rooster #99 $5
❏ 1985-86 Oilers
  Red Rooster #99 $5
❏ 1985-86 Oilers
  Red Rooster #99 $5
❏ 1985-86 Topps #120 $20
❏ 1985-86 Topps Box
  Bottoms #G $18
❏ 1985-86 Topps
  Sticker Inserts #2 $12
❏ 1986-87 Kraft Drawings #23 $25
❏ 1986-87 O-Pee-Chee #3 $25
❏ 1986-87 O-Pee-Chee #259 LL $6
❏ 1986-87 O-Pee-Chee #260 LL $6
❏ 1986-87 O-Pee-Chee Box
  Bottoms #F $15
❏ 1986-87 O-Pee-Chee Stickers
  #72 $2.50
❏ 1986-87 O-Pee-Chee Stickers
  #115 Foil w/ Petr Klima (129) $3
❏ 1986-87 O-Pee-Chee Stickers #183
  Foil w/ Larry Robinson (123) $3
❏ 1986-87 O-Pee-Chee Stickers
  #191 w/ Mike Liut (52) $3
❏ 1986-87 O-Pee-Chee Stickers
  #195 w/ Ray Ferraro (57) $3
❏ 1986-87 Oilers
  Red Rooster #99 $5
❏ 1986-87 Oilers
  Red Rooster #99 $5
❏ 1986-87 Oilers
  Team Issue #99 $12
❏ 1986-87 Topps #3 $18
❏ 1986-87 Topps Box
  Bottoms #F $15
❏ 1986-87 Topps
  Sticker Inserts #3 $10
❏ 1987-88 Gatineau Hull
  Olympiques #99 $20
❏ 1987-88 O-Pee-Chee #53 $20
❏ 1987-88 O-Pee-Chee Box
  Bottoms #A $10
❏ 1987-88 O-Pee-Chee
  Minis #13 $6
❏ 1987-88 O-Pee-Chee
  Stickers #86 $3
❏ 1987-88 O-Pee-Chee Stickers
  #115 w/ Shayne Corson (127) $2
❏ 1987-88 O-Pee-Chee Stickers
  #174 w/ Mark Howe (176) $2
❏ 1987-88 O-Pee-Chee Stickers
  #180 w/ Mike Bullard (37) $2
❏ 1987-88 O-Pee-Chee Stickers
  #181 w/ Neil Sheehy (38) $2
❏ 1987-88 Oilers
  Team Issue #99 $12
❏ 1987-88 Panini
  Stickers #192 $3.50
❏ 1987-88 Panini Stickers #197 $1
❏ 1987-88 Panini Stickers #198 $1
❏ 1987-88 Panini Stickers #199 $1
❏ 1987-88 Panini Stickers #200 $1
❏ 1987-88 Panini Stickers #261 $3.50
❏ 1987-88 Panini Stickers #371 $2.50
❏ 1987-88 Panini Stickers #373 $2.50
❏ 1987-88 Panini Stickers #389 $2.50
❏ 1987-88 Sault Ste. Marie
  Greyhounds #29 $75

❏ 1987-88 Topps #53 $15
❏ 1987-88 Topps
  Box Bottoms #A $10
❏ 1987-88 Topps
  Sticker Inserts #5 $7.50
❏ 1988-89 Esso All-Stars #15 $3
❏ 1988-89 Kings Smokey #11 $15
❏ 1988-89 O-Pee-Chee #120 $18
❏ 1988-89 O-Pee-Chee
  Box Bottoms #B $6

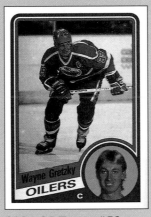

1984-85 Topps #51

❏ 1988-89 O-Pee-Chee
  Minis #11 $6
❏ 1988-89 O-Pee-Chee
  Stickers #1 MVP $2.50
❏ 1988-89 O-Pee-Chee Stickers
  #121 w/ Petr Klima (251) $2
❏ 1988-89 O-Pee-Chee
  Stickers #224 $2.50
❏ 1988-89 Oilers Tenth
  Anniversary #46 $20
❏ 1988-89 Oilers Tenth
  Anniversary #55 1050th $10
❏ 1988-89 Oilers Tenth Anniversary #137 Stanley Cup $7.50
❏ 1988-89 Panini
  Stickers #58 $2.50
❏ 1988-89 Panini
  Stickers #178 $.15
❏ 1988-89 Panini
  Stickers #181 $2.50
❏ 1988-89 Panini
  Stickers #193 $2.50
❏ 1988-89 Topps #120 $30
❏ 1988-89 Topps
  Box Bottoms #B $6
❏ 1988-89 Topps
  Sticker Inserts #8 $5
❏ 1989 Sports Illustrated
  For Kids #19 $7
❏ 1989-90 Action Packed
  Prototypes #1 $175
❏ 1989-90 Kings Smokey #1 $10
❏ 1989-90 Kings Smokey Gretzky
  8-by-10 #NNO $15
❏ 1989-90 Kraft #59 AS $8
❏ 1989-90 Kraft All-Stars Stickers
  #2 w/ Rick Tocchet $7
❏ 1989-90 O-Pee-Chee
  #156 $1.50
❏ 1989-90 O-Pee-Chee
  #320 AW $.75
❏ 1989-90 O-Pee-Chee
  #325 HL $.75

❏ 1989-90 O-Pee-Chee
  Box Bottoms #E $2
❏ 1989-90 O-Pee-Chee
  Sticker Back Cards #30 $3
❏ 1989-90 O-Pee-Chee
  Stickers #154 $1.50
❏ 1989-90 O-Pee-Chee
  Stickers #166 w/
  Randy Burridge (28) $1
❏ 1989-90 O-Pee-Chee
  Stickers #209 AW w/
  Doug Lidster $1.25
❏ 1989-90 Panini Stickers #87 $2
❏ 1989-90 Panini
  Stickers #179 AS $1
❏ 1989-90 Panini
  Stickers #374 $1.50
❏ 1989-90 Topps #156 $3
❏ 1989-90 Topps
  Box Bottoms #E $2
❏ 1989-90 Topps
  Insert Stickers #11 $3
❏ 1990-91 Bowman #143 $1.50
❏ 1990-91 Bowman
  Tiffany #143 $15
❏ 1990-91 Kings Smokey #1 $7.50
❏ 1990-91 Kraft #15 $8
❏ 1990-91 Kraft #66 AS $6
❏ 1990-91 O-Pee-Chee #1
  Indianapolis $.75
❏ 1990-91 O-Pee-Chee #2
  Edmonton $.60
❏ 1990-91 O-Pee-Chee #3
  Los Angeles $.60
❏ 1990-91 O-Pee-Chee #120 $1.50
❏ 1990-91 O-Pee-Chee
  #199 AS $.75

1995-96 Finest #5

❏ 1990-91 O-Pee-Chee
  #522 AW $.75
❏ 1990-91 O-Pee-Chee Box
  Bottoms #D $1.50
❏ 1990-91 OPC Premier #38 $5
❏ 1990-91 Panini
  Stickers #242 $1.50
❏ 1990-91 Panini
  Stickers #332 $1.50
❏ 1990-91 Pro Set #118 $.75
❏ 1990-91 Pro Set #340 AS $.35
❏ 1990-91 Pro Set #388 AW $.35
❏ 1990-91 Pro Set #394 LL $.35
❏ 1990-91 Pro Set #703
  2,000 Point $.50

❏ 1990-91 Pro Set Player of
  the Month #P2 $10
❏ 1990-91 Score #1 $1.25
❏ 1990-91 Score #321 AS $.35
❏ 1990-91 Score #336 Sniper $.35
❏ 1990-91 Score #338 Magic $.35
❏ 1990-91 Score #347 RB $.35
❏ 1990-91 Score #352 LL $.35
❏ 1990-91 Score #353 LL $.35
❏ 1990-91 Score #361 AW $.35
❏ 1990-91 Score Canadian
  #1 $1.25
❏ 1990-91 Score Canadian
  #321 AS $.35
❏ 1990-91 Score Canadian
  #336 Sniper $.35
❏ 1990-91 Score Canadian
  #338 Magic $.35
❏ 1990-91 Score Canadian
  #347 RB $.35
❏ 1990-91 Score Canadian
  #352 LL $.35
❏ 1990-91 Score Canadian
  #353 LL $.35
❏ 1990-91 Score Canadian
  #361 AW $.35
❏ 1990-91 Score Hottest/
  Rising Stars #1 $3
❏ 1990-91 Score Promos
  #1A ERR $60
❏ 1990-91 Score Promos
  #1B COR $25
❏ 1990-91 Score Rookie/Traded
  #110T 2,000th Point $1
❏ 1990-91 Topps
  #1 Indianapolis $.60
❏ 1990-91 Topps
  #2 Edmonton $.50
❏ 1990-91 Topps #3
  Los Angeles $.50
❏ 1990-91 Topps #120 $1.25
❏ 1990-91 Topps #199 AS $.60
❏ 1990-91 Topps
  Box Bottoms #D $1.50
❏ 1990-91 Topps Team Scoring
  Leaders #12 $2.50
❏ 1990-91 Topps Tiffany #1 $10
❏ 1990-91 Topps Tiffany #2 $10
❏ 1990-91 Topps Tiffany #3 $10
❏ 1990-91 Topps Tiffany
  #120 $15
❏ 1990-91 Topps Tiffany
  #199 AS $10
❏ 1990-91 Upper Deck #54 $2
❏ 1990-91 Upper Deck
  #205 AW $.75
❏ 1990-91 Upper Deck
  #307 TC $.75
❏ 1990-91 Upper Deck
  #476 AS $.75
❏ 1990-91 Upper Deck #545
  2000th Point $1
❏ 1990-91 Upper Deck French
  #54 $3
❏ 1990-91 Upper Deck French
  #205 AW $1.25
❏ 1990-91 Upper Deck French
  #307 TC $1.25
❏ 1990-91 Upper Deck French
  #476 AS $1.25
❏ 1990-91 Upper Deck French
  #545 2,000 Point $1.50
❏ 1990-91 Upper Deck

Holograms #1 $2
❏ 1990-91 Upper Deck
Holograms #2 $2
❏ 1990-91 Upper Deck
Holograms #3 $2
❏ 1990-91 Upper Deck
Promos #241A $30
❏ 1990-91 Upper Deck
Sheets #3 $15
❏ 1990-91 Upper Deck
Sheets #6 $15
❏ 1991 All World
(two prototypes) $25
❏ 1991 JL Productions Canada Cup
#1 Commemorative Sheet $10
❏ 1991Score National
/FanFest #1 $10
❏ 1991-92 Bowman #173 HT $.75
❏ 1991-92 Bowman #176 $1
❏ 1991-92 Kraft #65 $9
❏ 1991-92 OPC #201 HL $.50
❏ 1991-92 OPC #224 LL $.50
❏ 1991-92 OPC #257 LL $.50
❏ 1991-92 OPC #258 AS $.50
❏ 1991-92 OPC #321 $1
❏ 1991-92 OPC #520 AW $.50
❏ 1991-92 OPC #522 AW $.50
❏ 1991-92 OPC #524 HL $.50
❏ 1991-92 OPC Premier #3 $1.50

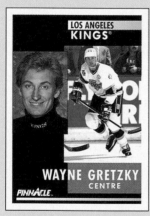

1991-92 Pinnacle #100

❏ 1991-92 Panini
Stickers #78 $1.50
❏ 1991-92 Panini Stickers #327 $1
❏ 1991-92 Parkhurst #73 $1.50
❏ 1991-92 Parkhurst #207
1,000 Point Club $1
❏ 1991-92 Parkhurst #222 AS $1
❏ 1991-92 Parkhurst #429 500
Goals Club $1
❏ 1991-92 Parkhurst #433 LL $1
❏ 1991-92 Parkhurst #465 AW $15
❏ 1991-92 Parkhurst
French #73 $1.50
❏ 1991-92 Parkhurst French
#207 1,000 Point Club $1
❏ 1991-92 Parkhurst French
#222 AS $1
❏ 1991-92 Parkhurst French #429
500 Goals Club $1
❏ 1991-92 Parkhurst French
#433 LL $1
❏ 1991-92 Parkhurst French
#465 AW $15
❏ 1991-92 Pinnacle #100 $2.50

❏ 1991-92 Pinnacle #381
Idol with Joe Sakic $1
❏ 1991-92 Pinnacle B #B11 $110
❏ 1991-92 Pinnacle B French
#B11 $125
❏ 1991-92 Pinnacle
French #100 $3
❏ 1991-92 Pinnacle French
#381 Idol with Joe Sakic $1.25
❏ 1991-92 Pro Set #101 $1
❏ 1991-92 Pro Set #285 AS $.50
❏ 1991-92 Pro Set #324 AW $.50
❏ 1991-92 Pro Set #574 CAPT $.50
❏ 1991-92 Pro Set CC #CC5 $5
❏ 1991-92 Pro Set French #101 $1
❏ 1991-92 Pro Set French
#285 AS $.50
❏ 1991-92 Pro Set French
#324 AW $.50
❏ 1991-92 Pro Set French
#574 CAPT $.50
❏ 1991-92 Pro Set NHL
Awards Special #AC4 $125
❏ 1991-92 Pro Set
Platinum #52 $1.25
❏ 1991-92 Pro Set
Platinum PC #PC4 $6
❏ 1991-92 Pro Set
Platinum PC #PC14 $6
❏ 1991-92 Pro Set
Puck Candy #11 $7.50
❏ 1991-92 Score
(promo 12th NSCC) #1 $8
❏ 1991-92 Score
(promo NCWA) #1 $8
❏ 1991-92 Score American
#100 $1
❏ 1991-92 Score American
#346 DT $.50
❏ 1991-92 Score American
#405 LL $.50
❏ 1991-92 Score American
#406 LL $.50
❏ 1991-92 Score American
#413 700 Goals $.50
❏ 1991-92 Score American
#422 FP $.50
❏ 1991-92 Score American
#427 AW $.50
❏ 1991-92 Score American
#434 AW $.50
❏ 1991-92 Score American
(promo) $
❏ 1991-92 Score Canadian
#100 $1
❏ 1991-92 Score Canadian
#295 LL $.50
❏ 1991-92 Score Canadian
#296 LL $.50
❏ 1991-92 Score Canadian
#303 700 Goals $.50
❏ 1991-92 Score Canadian
#312 FP $.50
❏ 1991-92 Score Canadian
#317 AW $.50
❏ 1991-92 Score Canadian
#324 AW $.50
❏ 1991-92 Score Canadian
#376 DT $.50
❏ 1991-92 Score Hot Cards #2 $9
❏ 1991-92 Semic-Slovart
Stickers #64 $10
❏ 1991-92 Stadium Club #1 $3

❏ 1991-92 Stadium Club Charter
Member 2,000 Pts NNO $3
❏ 1991-92 Stadium Club Charter
Member 700 Club NNO $3
❏ 1991-92 Topps #201 HL $.50
❏ 1991-92 Topps #224 LL $.50
❏ 1991-92 Topps #257 LL $.50
❏ 1991-92 Topps #258 AS $.50
❏ 1991-92 Topps #321 $1
❏ 1991-92 Topps #520 AW $.50
❏ 1991-92 Topps #522 AW $.50
❏ 1991-92 Topps #524 HL $.50
❏ 1991-92 Topps Team Scoring
Leaders #10 $2
❏ 1991-92 Topps/Bowman
Preview Sheet #2 $3
❏ 1991-92 Upper Deck #13 CC $1
❏ 1991-92 Upper Deck #38
Art Card $1
❏ 1991-92 Upper Deck #45
The 50/50 Club $.75
❏ 1991-92 Upper Deck #437 $1.50
❏ 1991-92 Upper Deck #501 CC
CL w/ Paul Coffey $.75
❏ 1991-92 Upper Deck
#621 AS $.75
❏ 1991-92 Upper Deck #SP1
w/ Hull and Kamensky $4
❏ 1991-92 Upper Deck Award
Winner Holograms #AW1 $2
❏ 1991-92 Upper Deck Award
Winner Holograms #AW6 $2
❏ 1991-92 Upper Deck Box
Bottoms #1 $2
❏ 1991-92 Upper Deck French
#13 CC $1
❏ 1991-92 Upper Deck French
#38 Art Card $1
❏ 1991-92 Upper Deck French
#45 The 50/50 Club $.75
❏ 1991-92 Upper Deck French
#437 $1.50
❏ 1991-92 Upper Deck French
#501 CC CL w/ Paul Coffey $.75
❏ 1991-92 Upper Deck French
#621 AS $.75
❏ 1991-92 Upper Deck French
#SP1 w/ Hull and Kamensky $4
❏ 1991-92 Upper Deck
McDonald's #17 $3
❏ 1991-92 Upper Deck
McDonald's #H1 $4
❏ 1991-92 Upper Deck
Sheets #1 $10
❏ 1991-92 Upper Deck
Sheets #8 $10
❏ 1991-92 Upper Deck World
Junior Tournament #NNO
Hologram 1 $4
❏ 1991-92 Upper Deck World
Junior Tournament #NNO
Hologram 2 $4
❏ 1992 Gartlan
Wayne Gretzky #1 $20
❏ 1992 High 5 Preview
Sample #P3 $50
❏ 1992 High-5 Previews #P1 $200
❏ 1992-93 Bowman #1 $7.50
❏ 1992-93 Bowman #207 FOIL
$15
❏ 1992-93 Humpty Dumpty I
#10 $5
❏ 1992-93 Kraft #40 AS $7

❏ 1992-93 O-Pee-Chee #15 $1.25
❏ 1992-93 O-Pee-Chee #220
Anniversary Tribute Card
(79-80) $3.50
❏ 1992-93 O-Pee-Chee 25th
Anniv. Inserts #12 $4
❏ 1992-93 Panini Stickers #64 $1
❏ 1992-93 Panini Stickers
#287 AS $1
❏ 1992-93 Parkhurst #65 $1.50
❏ 1992-93 Parkhurst #509 SCP $4
❏ 1992-93 Parkhurst Emerald Ice
#65 $7.50
❏ 1992-93 Parkhurst Emerald Ice
#509 SCP $20
❏ 1992-93 Parkhurst French #65 $2

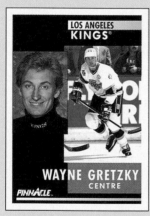

1994-95 TSC #99

❏ 1992-93 Parkhurst French
#509 SCP $5
❏ 1992-93 Parkhurst French
Emerald Ice #65 $10
❏ 1992-93 Parkhurst French
Emerald Ice #509 $25
❏ 1992-93 Pinnacle #200 $2
❏ 1992-93 Pinnacle #249 Idols
w/ Petr Nedved $1
❏ 1992-93 Pinnacle
French #200 $2.50
❏ 1992-93 Pinnacle French #249
Idols w/ Petr Nedved $1.25
❏ 1992-93 Pinnacle Team
Pinnacle #5 w/ Eric Lindros $35
❏ 1992-93 Pinnacle Team
Pinnacle French #5 w/
Eric Lindros $40
❏ 1992-93 Pro Set #66 $1.25
❏ 1992-93 Pro Set #246 LL $.75
❏ 1992-93 Pro Set Gold
Team Leaders #6 $12
❏ 1992-93 Score #1 $1.25
❏ 1992-93 Score #412 SL $.50
❏ 1992-93 Score #426 FP $.50
❏ 1992-93 Score #525 AW $.50
❏ 1992-93 Score Canadian #1 $1.25
❏ 1992-93 Score Canadian
#412 SL $.50
❏ 1992-93 Score Canadian
#426 FP $.50
❏ 1992-93 Score Canadian
#525 AW $.50
❏ 1992-93 Seasons Patches #9 $8
❏ 1992-93 Stadium Club #18 $2
❏ 1992-93 Stadium Club
#256 MC $1.50
❏ 1992-93 Topps #1 $1.25

- 1992-93 Topps #123 LL $.75
- 1992-93 Topps Gold #1G $45
- 1992-93 Topps Gold #123G LL $18
- 1992-93 Topps Stadium Members Only Always a Gentleman $2
- 1992-93 Ultra #83 $2
- 1992-93 Ultra All-Stars #10 $8
- 1992-93 Ultra Award Winners #6 $8
- 1992-93 Upper Deck #25 $1.50
- 1992-93 Upper Deck #33 1,500 Points $.75
- 1992-93 Upper Deck #37 Brothers w/ Keith and Brent $.75
- 1992-93 Upper Deck #423 w/ Brett Hull $.75
- 1992-93 Upper Deck #435 AW $.75
- 1992-93 Upper Deck #621 PRO $.75
- 1992-93 Upper Deck All-World Team #W1 $8
- 1992-93 Upper Deck French #25 $2
- 1992-93 Upper Deck French #37 BL $1
- 1992-93 Upper Deck French #423 Multiplayer $1
- 1992-93 Upper Deck French #435 AW $1
- 1992-93 Upper Deck French #621 $1
- 1992-93 Upper Deck Gordie Howe Heroes #26 $3

1992-93 Score #525

- 1992-93 Upper Deck Gordie Howe Selects #G5 $12
- 1992-93 Upper Deck Wayne Gretzky Heroes Set 9 cards plus header $45
- 1992-93 Upper Deck World Junior Grads #WG10 $20
- 1993 "Face to Face" #580 board card game $5
- 1993 Hockey Wit #99 $2
- 1993 NHL All-Star Game Commemorative #4 Multiplayer $5
- 1993 Sports Illustrated For Kids #153 $5
- 1993 Upper Deck Locker All-Stars #25 $2
- 1993 Upper Deck Soccer World

- Cup #HC4 Honorary Captain $10
- 1993 Upper Deck Soccer World Cup (gold) #HC4 Honorary Captain (gold foil) $30
- 1993-94 Donruss #152 $2
- 1993-94 Donruss #395 RB w/ Lub Robitaille $1
- 1993-94 Donruss Elite #10 $80
- 1993-94 Donruss Ice Kings #4 $6
- 1993-94 Donruss Special Print #K $20
- 1993-94 Great Western Forum #10 (25th Anniversary Set) $5
- 1993-94 Highland Mint Topps #5 Bronze $75
- 1993-94 Highland Mint Topps #5 Silver $375
- 1993-94 Kraft #34 $8
- 1993-94 Kraft #54 $5
- 1993-94 Kraft Captains disc #NNO $5
- 1993-94 Kraft Jello #NNO $5
- 1993-94 Leaf #304 $2
- 1993-94 Leaf Gold All-Stars #6 w/ Doug Gilmour $15
- 1993-94 Leaf Studio Signature #4 $12
- 1993-94 O-Pee-Chee Premier Gold #330 $10
- 1993-94 O-Pee-Chee Premier Gold #380 CAN $10
- 1993-94 OPC Premier #330 $1.25
- 1993-94 OPC Premier #380 CAN $1
- 1993-94 OPC Premier Black Gold #1 $25
- 1993-94 Panini #R $3
- 1993-94 Parkhurst #99 $1.50
- 1993-94 Parkhurst Cherry's Playoff Heroes #D1 $80
- 1993-94 Parkhurst East/West Stars #W1 $55
- 1993-94 Parkhurst Emerald Ice #99 $9
- 1993-94 Parkhurst USA/Canada Gold #G1 $30
- 1993-94 Pinnacle #237 NT $1.50
- 1993-94 Pinnacle #400 $2
- 1993-94 Pinnacle #512 HL $8
- 1993-94 Pinnacle All-Stars #45 $1.50
- 1993-94 Pinnacle All-Stars Canadian #45 $1.50
- 1993-94 Pinnacle Canadian #237 NT $1.50
- 1993-94 Pinnacle Canadian #400 $2
- 1993-94 Pinnacle Canadian #512 HL $8
- 1993-94 Pinnacle Captains #11 $35
- 1993-94 Pinnacle Captains Canadian #11 $40
- 1993-94 Pinnacle Team Pinnacle #5 w/ Mario Lemieux $100
- 1993-94 Pinnacle Team Pinnacle Canadian #5 w/ Mario Lemieux $125
- 1993-94 PowerPlay #116 $3
- 1993-94 PowerPlay

- Gamebreakers #3 $7
- 1993-94 PowerPlay Point Leaders #3 $6
- 1993-94 Score #300 $1
- 1993-94 Score #662 802 Goals $2.50
- 1993-94 Score Dream Team #11 $30
- 1993-94 Score Dynamic Duos U.S. #7 w/ Jari Kurri $60
- 1993-94 Score Franchise #9 $30
- 1993-94 Score Gold #300 $6
- 1993-94 Score Gold #662 802 Goals $15
- 1993-94 Seasons Patches #5 $7.50
- 1993-94 Stadium Club #200 $1.50
- 1993-94 Stadium Club All-Stars #23 w/ Mario Lemieux $40
- 1993-94 Stadium Club Finest #1 $15
- 1993-94 Stadium Club First Day Issue #200 $200
- 1993-94 Stadium Club Master Photos #8 $7
- 1993-94 Stadium Club Master Photos #8 Winner Expired $8.50
- 1993-94 Stadium Club OPC #200 $1.50
- 1993-94 Topps #330 $1.25
- 1993-94 Topps #380 CAN $1
- 1993-94 Topps Premier Black Gold #7 $10
- 1993-94 Topps Premier Black Gold #A Winner Expired $4
- 1993-94 Topps Premier Gold #330 $8
- 1993-94 Topps Premier Gold #380 $8
- 1993-94 Topps Stadium Master Photo Winner $5
- 1993-94 Ultra #114 $2
- 1993-94 Ultra #C3C Wayne Gretzky 2/10 $8
- 1993-94 Ultra All-Stars #15 $10
- 1993-94 Ultra Premier Pivots #2 $7
- 1993-94 Ultra Scoring Kings #2 $10
- 1993-94 Upper Deck #99 $1.50
- 1993-94 Upper Deck #99 802 Gold $10
- 1993-94 Upper Deck #99 802 Silver $25
- 1993-94 Upper Deck Authenticated #802 $25
- 1993-94 Upper Deck Gretzky Box Bottom #1 $1
- 1993-94 Upper Deck Gretzky Sheet #1 $20
- 1993-94 Upper Deck Next In Line #NL1 w/ Michael Nylander $8
- 1993-94 Upper Deck NHL's Best #HB9 $40
- 1993-94 Upper Deck Silver Skates #R1 $25
- 1993-94 Upper Deck Silver Skates #NNO Gold Trade $80
- 1993-94 Upper Deck Silver Skates #NNO Silver Trade $35

- 1993-94 Upper Deck Silver Skates Retail Gold #RG1 $35
- 1993-94 Upper Deck SP #70 Wayne Gretzky $10
- 1993-94 Upper Deck W. Gretzky Promo #99 $2
- 1994 Coke/Mac's Milk Gretzky POGs Set 18 cards $15

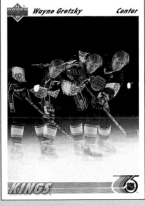

1991-92 Upper Deck #437

- 1994 EA Sports #63 Wayne Gretzky $10
- 1994 EA Sports #192 SK. L $6
- 1994 Hockey Wit #99 $3.50
- 1994 JAA Kiekko #99 $10
- 1994 JAA Kiekko #344 DT $10
- 1994 Stadium Club Members Only #5 $4
- 1994 Upper Deck Gretzky 24K Gold #1 $150
- 1994 Upper Deck NHLPA /Be A Player #7 $4
- 1994 Upper Deck Soccer World Cup #C8 Honorary Captain (English/Spanish) $75
- 1994 Upper Deck Soccer World Cup #C8 Honorary Captain (English/Japanese) $100
- 1994-95 Be A Player #R99 TT $4
- 1994-95 Be A Player #R147 DLO $4
- 1994-95 Be A Player #R176 FAN $4
- 1994-95 Be A Player 99 All-Star #G1 $70
- 1994-95 Be A Player Signature Cards #108 $1,200
- 1994-95 Be A Player Up Close and Personal #UC1 $30
- 1994-95 Donruss #127 $2
- 1994-95 Donruss Dominators #5 w/ Roenick and Fedorov $25
- 1994-95 Donruss Elite #5 $70
- 1994-95 Donruss Ice Masters #4 $8
- 1994-95 Finest #41 $8
- 1994-95 Finest Division's Finest Clear Cut #18 $30
- 1994-95 Finest Refractors #41 $300
- 1994-95 Finest Ring Leaders #5 $75
- 1994-95 Finest Super Team Winners #41 $25

- ❏ 1994-95 Flair #79 $5
- ❏ 1994-95 Flair Center Spotlight #4 $10
- ❏ 1994-95 Flair Hot Numbers #2 $40
- ❏ 1994-95 Fleer #94 $2
- ❏ 1994-95 Fleer Headliners #4 $5
- ❏ 1994-95 Kraft #5 $5
- ❏ 1994-95 Kraft #63 $6
- ❏ 1994-95 Leaf #345 $5
- ❏ 1994-95 Leaf Fire on Ice #4 $10
- ❏ 1994-95 Leaf Gold Stars #1 w/ Sergei Fedorov $90

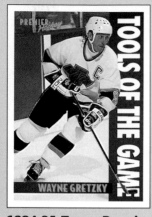

1994-95 Topps Premier #280

- ❏ 1994-95 Leaf Limited #10 $8
- ❏ 1994-95 Leaf Limited Gold #7 $150
- ❏ 1994-95 Leaf Limited Inserts #11 $20
- ❏ 1994-95 OPC Premier #130 AS $1.25
- ❏ 1994-95 OPC Premier #150 LL $1.25
- ❏ 1994-95 OPC Premier #154 LL $1.25
- ❏ 1994-95 OPC Premier #280 TOTG $1.25
- ❏ 1994-95 OPC Premier #375 $2.25
- ❏ 1994-95 OPC Premier Special Effects #130 AS $22.50
- ❏ 1994-95 OPC Premier Special Effects #150 LL $22.50
- ❏ 1994-95 OPC Premier Special Effects #154 LL $22.50
- ❏ 1994-95 OPC Premier Special Effects #280 TOTG $22.50
- ❏ 1994-95 OPC Premier Special Effects #375 $40
- ❏ 1994-95 OPC Premier The Go To Guy #1 $25
- ❏ 1994-95 Parkhurst #103 $1.50
- ❏ 1994-95 Parkhurst #306 PB $1
- ❏ 1994-95 Parkhurst Crash The Game Blue #11 $12
- ❏ 1994-95 Parkhurst Crash The Game Blue #28 Western Conf. $12
- ❏ 1994-95 Parkhurst Crash The Game Gold #11 $3
- ❏ 1994-95 Parkhurst Crash The Game Gold #28 Western Conf. $3

- ❏ 1994-95 Parkhurst Crash The Game Green #11 $12
- ❏ 1994-95 Parkhurst Crash The Game Green #28 Western Conf. $12
- ❏ 1994-95 Parkhurst Crash The Game Red #11 $12
- ❏ 1994-95 Parkhurst Crash The Game Red #28 Western Conf. $12
- ❏ 1994-95 Parkhurst Gold #103 $100
- ❏ 1994-95 Parkhurst Gold #306 PB $70
- ❏ 1994-95 Parkhurst SE #NNO 4-by-6 card (UD#226) $5
- ❏ 1994-95 Parkhurst SE Vintage #20 $12
- ❏ 1994-95 Pinnacle #200 $2
- ❏ 1994-95 Pinnacle Artist's Proofs #200 $500
- ❏ 1994-95 Pinnacle Rink Collection #200 $50
- ❏ 1994-95 Pinnacle Team Pinnacle #TP9 w/ Mark Messier $100
- ❏ 1994-95 Post Cereal Box Backs #13 $10
- ❏ 1994-95 Score #241 HL $1
- ❏ 1994-95 Score 90 Plus Club #1 $30
- ❏ 1994-95 Score Dream Team #DT14 $30
- ❏ 1994-95 Score Franchise #TF11 $100
- ❏ 1994-95 Score Gold #241 HL $12
- ❏ 1994-95 Score Platinum Team Sets #241 HL $50
- ❏ 1994-95 Select #83 $2
- ❏ 1994-95 Select First Line #11 $60
- ❏ 1994-95 Select Gold #83 $45
- ❏ 1994-95 SP #54 $5
- ❏ 1994-95 SP #SP1 2,500 Points $90
- ❏ 1994-95 SP Die-Cuts #54 $15
- ❏ 1994-95 SP Premier #17 $20
- ❏ 1994-95 SP Premier Die-Cuts #17 $200
- ❏ 1994-95 Stadium Club #99 $2
- ❏ 1994-95 Stadium Club #270 TW $1.50
- ❏ 1994-95 Stadium Club Finest Inserts #4 $20
- ❏ 1994-95 Stadium Club Super Team Winners #99 $10
- ❏ 1994-95 Stadium Club Super Team Winners #270 TW $7.50
- ❏ 1994-95 Topps Premier #130 AS $.75
- ❏ 1994-95 Topps Premier #150 LL $.75
- ❏ 1994-95 Topps Premier #154 LL $.75
- ❏ 1994-95 Topps Premier #280 TOTG $.75
- ❏ 1994-95 Topps Premier #375 $1.50
- ❏ 1994-95 Topps Premier Special Effects #130 AS $15
- ❏ 1994-95 Topps Premier Special Effects #150 LL $15

- ❏ 1994-95 Topps Premier Special Effects #154 LL $15
- ❏ 1994-95 Topps Premier Special Effects #280 TOTG $15
- ❏ 1994-95 Topps Premier Special Effects #375 $25
- ❏ 1994-95 Topps The Go To Guy #1 $25
- ❏ 1994-95 Ultra #306 $2.50
- ❏ 1994-95 Ultra All-Stars #10 $3
- ❏ 1994-95 Ultra Award Winners #5 $6
- ❏ 1994-95 Ultra Premier Pivots #4 $7
- ❏ 1994-95 Ultra Scoring Kings #4 $7
- ❏ 1994-95 Upper Deck #1 $2
- ❏ 1994-95 Upper Deck #226 802 Goals $2
- ❏ 1994-95 Upper Deck #228 SE $1.50
- ❏ 1994-95 Upper Deck #541 WT $1.50
- ❏ 1994-95 Upper Deck Electric Ice #1 $125
- ❏ 1994-95 Upper Deck Electric Ice #226 802 Goals $125
- ❏ 1994-95 Upper Deck Electric Ice #228 SE $100
- ❏ 1994-95 Upper Deck Electric Ice #541 WT $100
- ❏ 1994-95 Upper Deck Ice Gallery #IG15 $20
- ❏ 1994-95 Upper Deck Predictor Hart #H1 $20
- ❏ 1994-95 Upper Deck Predictor Hart #H1 Silver exchange $10
- ❏ 1994-95 Upper Deck Predictor Hart #H1 Gold Exchange $10
- ❏ 1994-95 Upper Deck Predictor Pearson/Norris #C16 $20

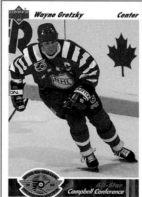

1991-92 Upper Deck #621

- ❏ 1994-95 Upper Deck Predictor Pearson/Norris #C16 Gold Exchange $10
- ❏ 1994-95 Upper Deck Predictor Playoff Scoring #R42 $20
- ❏ 1994-95 Upper Deck Predictor Playoff Scoring #R59 $20
- ❏ 1994-95 Upper Deck Predictor Playoff Scoring #R42 Gold Exchange $10
- ❏ 1994-95 Upper Deck Predictor

- ❏ Playoff Scoring #R59 Gold Exchange $10
- ❏ 1994-95 Upper Deck Predictor Ross/Vezina #H16 $20
- ❏ 1994-95 Upper Deck Predictor Ross/Vezina #H16 Gold Exchange $10
- ❏ 1994-95 Upper Deck Predictor Scoring #R19 $20
- ❏ 1994-95 Upper Deck Predictor Scoring #R21 $20
- ❏ 1994-95 Upper Deck Predictor Scoring #R19 Gold Exchange $10
- ❏ 1994-95 Upper Deck Predictor Scoring #R21 Gold Exchange $10
- ❏ 1994-95 Upper Deck SP Inserts #SP36 $10
- ❏ 1994-95 Upper Deck SP Inserts Die-Cuts #SP36 $50
- ❏ 1995 Canada Games NHL POGS #126 $10
- ❏ 1995 Canada Games NHL POGS #268 AS $10
- ❏ 1995 Finnish Semic World Championships #99 $10
- ❏ 1995 Globe World Champi- onships #99 $10
- ❏ 1995 Globe World Champ- onships #265 SPEC $10
- ❏ 1995 Globe World Champi- onships #266 SPEC $10
- ❏ 1995 Globe World Champi- onships #267 SPEC $10
- ❏ 1995 Stadium Club Members Only #32 $2.50
- ❏ 1995-96 Be A Player #97 $6
- ❏ 1995-96 Be A Player Gretzky's Great Moments Set 10 Cards $135
- ❏ 1995-96 Be A Player Lethal Lines #LL2 $30
- ❏ 1995-96 Be A Player Signatures #S97 $700
- ❏ 1995-96 Be A Player Signatures #*S97 Die-Cut $1,800
- ❏ 1995-96 Bowman #1 $2
- ❏ 1995-96 Bowman All Foil #1 $20
- ❏ 1995-96 Bowman's Best #BB5 $25
- ❏ 1995-96 Bowman's Best Refractors #BB5 $150
- ❏ 1995-96 Collector's Choice #1 $1.25
- ❏ 1995-96 Collector's Choice #361 WYG $.60
- ❏ 1995-96 Collector's Choice #395 CL $.25
- ❏ 1995-96 Collector's Choice #396 CL $.25
- ❏ 1995-96 Collector's Choice Crash The Game #C3A Silver $4
- ❏ 1995-96 Collector's Choice Crash The Game #C3B Silver $4
- ❏ 1995-96 Collector's Choice Crash The Game #C3C Silver $4
- ❏ 1995-96 Collector's Choice Crash The Game #C3A Gold $15
- ❏ 1995-96 Collector's Choice Crash The Game #C3BGold $15
- ❏ 1995-96 Collector's Choice

Crash The Game #C3C Gold $15
- [ ] 1995-96 Collector's Choice
Crash The Game #C3
Redeemed Silver $4
- [ ] 1995-96 Collector's Choice
Plat.Player's Club #1 $140
- [ ] 1995-96 Collector's Choice
Plat.Player's Club #361 WYG $80
- [ ] 1995-96 Collector's Choice
Plat.Player's Club #395 CL $25
- [ ] 1995-96 Collector's Choice
Plat.Player's Club #396 CL $25
- [ ] 1995-96 Collector's Choice
Player's Club #1 $12.50
- [ ] 1995-96 Collector's Choice
Player's Club #361 $7
- [ ] 1995-96 Collector's Choice
Player's Club #395 CL $2.50
- [ ] 1995-96 Collector's Choice
Player's Club #396 CL $2.50
- [ ] 1995-96 Donruss #13 $2
- [ ] 1995-96 Donruss Dominators

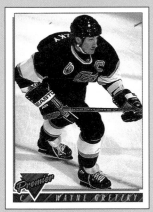

1993-94 Topps/OPC Premier #330

#5 w/ Gilmour and Fedorov $50
- [ ] 1995-96 Donruss Elite #58 $5
- [ ] 1995-96 Donruss Elite
Cutting Edge #3 $80
- [ ] 1995-96 Donruss Elite
Die-Cut Stars #58 $175
- [ ] 1995-96 Donruss Elite
Inserts #7 $60
- [ ] 1995-96 Emotion #81 $8
- [ ] 1995-96 Emotion Xcel #4 $90
- [ ] 1995-96 Emotion Xcited #5 $10
- [ ] 1995-96 Finest #5 Bronze $9
- [ ] 1995-96 Finest #180 Gold $125
- [ ] 1995-96 Finest Refractors
#5 Bronze $175
- [ ] 1995-96 Finest Refractors
#180 Gold $1,250
- [ ] 1995-96 Fleer Metal #71 $3.50
- [ ] 1995-96 Fleer Metal Heavy
Metal #4 $40
- [ ] 1995-96 Fleer Metal
International Steel #5 $10
- [ ] 1995-96 Leaf #89 $2
- [ ] 1995-96 Leaf Fire On Ice #10 $50
- [ ] 1995-96 Leaf Limited #87 $9
- [ ] 1995-96 Leaf Limited
Stars of the Game #3 $60
- [ ] 1995-96 NHL Aces Playing
Cards #1D $3
- [ ] 1995-96 NHL Cool Trade #2 $4

- [ ] 1995-96 NHL Cool Trade
enhanced redemption #2 $10
- [ ] 1995-96 Parkhurst Int'l Crown
Coll.Silver Ser.1 #6 $30
- [ ] 1995-96 Parkhurst Int'l Crown
Coll.Gold Ser.1 #6 $120
- [ ] 1995-96 Parkhurst Int'l Crown
Coll.Silver Ser.2 #10 $30
- [ ] 1995-96 Parkhurst Int'l Crown
Coll.Gold Ser.2 #10 $120
- [ ] 1995-96 Parkhurst
International #100 $2
- [ ] 1995-96 Parkhurst
International #449 $4
- [ ] 1995-96 Parkhurst International
Emerald Ice #100 $50
- [ ] 1995-96 Parkhurst International
Emerald Ice #449 $75
- [ ] 1995-96 Parkhurst International
NHL All-Stars #1 w/ Mario
Lemieux $125
- [ ] 1995-96 Pinnacle #101 $2
- [ ] 1995-96 Pinnacle Artist's Proofs
#101 $425
- [ ] 1995-96 Pinnacle Clear Shots
#9 $40
- [ ] 1995-96 Pinnacle Fantasy #13
$10
- [ ] 1995-96 Pinnacle First Strike #2
$50
- [ ] 1995-96 Pinnacle Rink Collection #101 $50
- [ ] 1995-96 Playoff One on One
#50 $3
- [ ] 1995-96 Playoff One on One
#159 $5
- [ ] 1995-96 Playoff One on One
#269 URB $200
- [ ] 1995-96 Score #250 $1.25
- [ ] 1995-96 Score Artist's Proofs
#250 $200
- [ ] 1995-96 Score Border Battle #2
$10
- [ ] 1995-96 Score Dream Team #1
$40
- [ ] 1995-96 Score Lamplighters #1
$40
- [ ] 1995-96 Select Certified #23 $8
- [ ] 1995-96 Select Certified Gold
Team #2 $125
- [ ] 1995-96 Select Certified
Mirror Gold #23 $125
- [ ] 1995-96 SkyBox Impact
#79 $1.25
- [ ] 1995-96 SkyBox Impact
Countdown to Impact #4 $45
- [ ] 1995-96 SkyBox Impact
Ice Quake #6 $25
- [ ] 1995-96 SP #127 $5
- [ ] 1995-96 SP #GC1 $150
- [ ] 1995-96 SP Holoviews
#FX10 $25
- [ ] 1995-96 SP Holoviews
#FX10 FX $150
- [ ] 1995-96 SP Stars/Etoiles
#E17 $12
- [ ] 1995-96 SP Stars/Etoiles
Gold #E17 $125
- [ ] 1995-96 Stadium Club
#173 EC $7
- [ ] 1995-96 Stadium Club
Metalists #M1 $55
- [ ] 1995-96 Stadium Club Nemeses

#N2 w/ Mario Lemieux $45
- [ ] 1995-96 Summit #24 $2
- [ ] 1995-96 Summit Artist's
Proof #24 $325
- [ ] 1995-96 Summit GM's
Choice #18 $60
- [ ] 1995-96 Summit Ice #24 $45
- [ ] 1995-96 Topps #85 $1.25

1991-92 Upper Deck #13

- [ ] 1995-96 Topps #375 MM $.75
- [ ] 1995-96 Topps Home Grown
Canada #HGC20 $100
- [ ] 1995-96 Topps Marquee Men
Power Boosters #375 $30
- [ ] 1995-96 Topps Mystery Finest
#M1 $30
- [ ] 1995-96 Topps Mystery Finest
Refractor #M1 $150
- [ ] 1995-96 Topps OPC
Inserts #85 $15
- [ ] 1995-96 Topps OPC
Inserts #375 MM $40
- [ ] 1995-96 Topps
Profiles #PF1 $15
- [ ] 1995-96 Topps Rink Leaders
#10RL $30
- [ ] 1995-96 Topps SuperSkills
#15 PC $4
- [ ] 1995-96 Ultra #74 $2
- [ ] 1995-96 Ultra #385 UC $3
- [ ] 1995-96 Ultra Extra
Attackers #7 $40
- [ ] 1995-96 Ultra Gold
Medallion #74 $20
- [ ] 1995-96 Ultra Premier
Pivots #3 $10
- [ ] 1995-96 Ultra Premier
Pivots #3 Gold Medallion $30
- [ ] 1995-96 Ultra Ultraview
#2 $40
- [ ] 1995-96 Ultra Ultraview #2
Hot Pack $28
- [ ] 1995-96 Upper Deck #99 $2
- [ ] 1995-96 Upper Deck #222 5 $1
- [ ] 1995-96 Upper Deck
#252 MM $1
- [ ] 1995-96 Upper Deck Cool Trade
Exchange card #NNO w/
Forsberg, Gilmour,
Fedorov $4
- [ ] 1995-96 Upper Deck
Electric Ice #99 $15
- [ ] 1995-96 Upper Deck

Electric Ice #222 5 $9
- [ ] 1995-96 Upper Deck
Electric Ice #252 MM $9
- [ ] 1995-96 Upper Deck
Freeze Frame #F2 $35
- [ ] 1995-96 Upper Deck
Gold Electric Ice #99 $175
- [ ] 1995-96 Upper Deck
Gold Electric Ice #222 $100
- [ ] 1995-96 Upper Deck
Gold Electric Ice #252 $100
- [ ] 1995-96 Upper Deck NHL
All-Stars #AS5
w/ Mario Lemieux $50
- [ ] 1995-96 Upper Deck NHL
All-Stars #AS5 Jumbo
w/ Mario Lemieux $60
- [ ] 1995-96 Upper Deck Pred.
Ross/Pearson/Smythe #R31 $25
- [ ] 1995-96 Upper Deck Pred.
Ross/Pearson/Smythe #R41 $25
- [ ] 1995-96 Upper Deck Pred.
Ross/Pearson/Smythe #R51 $25
- [ ] 1995-96 Upper Deck Predictor
Hart/Vezina #H7 $25
- [ ] 1995-96 Upper Deck Predictor
Scoring #R13 $25
- [ ] 1995-96 Upper Deck Predictor
Scoring #R23 $25
- [ ] 1995-96 Upper Deck Record
Collection Set 24 cards $180
- [ ] 1995-96 Upper Deck Special
Edition #SE128 $10
- [ ] 1995-96 Upper Deck Special
Edition Gold #SE128 $75
- [ ] 1995-96 Zenith #13 $9
- [ ] 1995-96 Zenith
Z-Team #4 $250
- [ ] 1995-96 Collector's Choice
Crash the Game #C3
redeemed Gold $10
- [ ] 1995-96 Collector's Choice
Crash the Game #C3 Gold
Bonus card $20

1995-96 Score #250

- [ ] 1996 Semic Wien #99 $10
- [ ] 1996 Upper Deck ASG MVP
Predictor $20
- [ ] 1996 Upper Deck ASG MVP
Predictor gold redeemed
card $30
- [ ] 1995-96 Post Upper Deck $10
- [ ] 1995-96 Post Upper Deck
Autographed version $1,500

Hall of WAYNE

One of the best collections of hockey memorabilia — outside of the Hall of Fame, of course — can be found at Wayne Gretzky's restaurant

By Jim Stevens

While a tour through the Hockey Hall of Fame is a must for any hockey fan when visiting Toronto, a new "must-see" stop for even the most casual of hockey followers was added to the city when Wayne Gretzky's restaurant opened on Aug. 17, 1993.

The display of hockey memorabilia at Gretzky's favorite eatery is spectacular — in terms not just of quality, but quantity and presentation. It compares favorably to the memorabilia on display in another superstar's restaurant, Larry Bird's Hotel and Restaurant in Terre Haute, Ind. The design and presentation of Wayne's treasures, however, is far superior to that of the Boston Celtics' great.

The person responsible for designing both the restaurant and the memorabilia displays is Gordon MacKay of MacKay & Wong Architects, whose offices happen to be directly above Gretzky's. As a lifelong hockey fan, MacKay was thrilled when his firm was selected for the project. He says the arrangement of the memorabilia is very specific.

"In the bar area, we tried to basically focus on Wayne's friends, mostly celebrities — not only in the sports world, but in the entertainment world as well," MacKay says. "We rotate those displays on a seasonal basis, encompassing not only the four major sports, but other sports such as tennis, auto racing and skiing."

The front of Gretzky's restaurant is a neon beacon for hockey enthusiasts.

MacKay says Wayne and his agent, Michael Barnett, furnished most of the memorabilia pieces. The pieces themselves were acquired in various ways — either by donation, through a loan or exchanged via trade involving Wayne's personal mementos.

"We do approach other athletes when they visit the restaurant to see if they would like to loan some artifacts," MacKay adds. "For instance, when figure skaters Brian Orser and Kurt Browning came into the restaurant last year, I spoke to them and within a month, we had some items from them to display. Another time, the entire McLaren racing team came into the restaurant during the Molson Indy

race, and within a week we had some great stuff — including the helmet Ayrton Senna wore in the race before he died."

As you head toward the bar area, the memorabilia immediately catches your attention: helmets, shoes and other equipment worn by the likes of Troy Aikman, Jim Kelly, Ozzie Smith, Orel Hershiser, Roberto Alomar, Bo Jackson, Guy Lafleur, Theo Fleury, Brett Hull and Michael Jordan. Among the most unusual items is the infamous Marty McSorley stick that cost Wayne's Los Angeles Kings the second game of the 1993 Stanley Cup finals. Also on display are a pair of Air Jordan shoes that Wayne received as a Christmas gift. Gretzky and Jordan have exchanged footwear as holiday gifts a number of times.

Another impressive display contains jerseys worn by Gretzky (from the 1987 Canada Cup) and Vladislav Tretiak, the legendary Soviet goaltender, and one worn by a Swedish national player. That display is topped by a 1977 Team Canada signed stick. Rounding out the memorabilia in the bar are two of Wayne's All-Star Game jerseys and numerous trophies and awards won by The Great One.

Once you exit the bar and approach the dining section, the memorabilia details more of Gretzky's life and achievements.

"The rest of the restaurant predominantly focuses on Wayne's career, not only from a hockey standpoint, but a bit of his family as well," MacKay says. "One display case focuses on Wayne's business and off - ice ventures, including his endorsements and his horse racing and collecting hobbies."

One highlight used to be the Honus Wagner baseball card that Wayne and former Kings owner Bruce McNall paid a record $451,000 for at an auction several years ago. Wayne has since sold the card to Treat Entertainment, and it was the grand prize in Treat Entertainment and Wal-Mart's "The World's Most Valuable Card Giveaway" contest. Other items on display are a Pro Stars cereal box featuring Wayne on the front, a Wayne Gretzky Mattel doll; and cartoon cells picturing Gretzky with Bo Jackson, among others.

Another display provides a fascinating look at Wayne's childhood, especially on-ice.

"When we were putting the artifacts together, we went out to Wayne's parents' home in Brantford and went through a lot of the family-oriented pieces," MacKay explains. "A case focusing on Wayne's family includes various trophies and medals won by each of Wayne's brothers and sisters. Also included is a family photo album, which is held open by a pair of

On the side of the restaurant building is a mural of Wayne and his dad.

Walter Gretzky's hockey gloves. I was also fortunate enough to go down to Wayne's house in Los Angeles and pick out a few more items to display at the restaurant."

Among the items are: the first pair of skates Wayne wore as a 2-year-old, a jersey he wore at age 9; and the entire season's score sheet from the Nadrofsky Steelers team of 1971-72. In that season, Wayne scored an incredible 378 goals and 517 points in 82 games. The team's record that year: 76-2-4.

Other cases feature Gretzky's Soo Greyhounds junior jersey, his first Indianapolis Racers jersey (his first pro team, for which he played just eight games before being sold to Edmonton); his Oilers WHA jersey, and his 1979 WHA All-Star Game jersey, a game in which Wayne fulfilled a dream by playing alongside his boyhood idol, Gordie Howe.

In the dining area, a huge glass-enclosed case displays 16 more significant sticks and pucks from Gretzky's long career. While these mementos are changed periodically, the case currently contains many of the sticks used to score the goals leading up to Wayne's NHL regular season career record of 802, which he set on March 23, 1994.

The private dining area contains

more treasures, highlighted by the 1940s Gordie Howe game-worn jersey that Wayne purchased for $27,000 at an auction a few years ago. Another wall displays Gretzky's rookie Edmonton Oilers jersey. Three other imposing jerseys also are hanging on the wall — Bobby Hull's WHA Winnipeg Jets jersey, Howe's WHA Houston Aeros jersey and Wayne's L.A. Kings Stanley Cup finals jersey from 1993.

Another artifact, which should be on display shortly, is the goal net in which Wayne deposited his record-setting goal No. 802. That net is a gift from Barnett.

Overall, the memorabilia at Gretzky's restaurant is just as good as the player whose name adorns the entrance.

"It's a real testament to Wayne," MacKay says. "From the very beginning, he was as helpful and resourceful as he possibly could be. When we went to his house, we basically went through everything he had in the living room. He was even pulling stuff off the mantelpiece."

And when Wayne finally reaches the Hall of Fame once his career is over, hockey fans who visit Toronto will have plenty of chances to see his memorabilia — in both places. •

Jim Stevens is a freelance writer based in Aurora, Colo.

ick Sheffler doesn't live in Aurora, Ill., but he's proudly produced his own version of Wayne's World just 40 miles to the north.

Owning one of the largest collections of Wayne Gretzky memorabilia on the planet, the Wheeling, Ill., police officer is skating through the recreational portion of his life by sticking to a firm policy: Have fun by collecting what you like.

Sheffler, 42, has collected Gretzky memorabilia for nearly a decade, and the enjoyment shows no signs of waning. An entire room of Sheffler's northwest suburban Chicago home is filled with Gretzky collectibles, while the other rooms feature a smaller number of items devoted to The Great One. Entry to Sheffler's den reveals autographed Gretzky pictures, posters and sticks mounted on the walls; game-worn jerseys hugging upper torso mannequins on a table; and commemorative medallions, game tickets, plates and pucks in clear glass hutches.

Sheffler estimates that he owns close to 2,500 Gretzky collectibles, including more than 600 different trading cards, 400 videotapes, 250 books, 200 magazine covers, 100 posters, 40 different T-shirts, six jerseys, four game-worn helmets and three pairs of gloves, plus figurines, lunch boxes, hats, pins, lithographs, pennants and patches — all associated with the man most hockey experts consider the greatest player in the history of the sport.

"Not only is he the No. 1 goal scorer in NHL history, but he's the best playmaker and passer I've ever seen," says Sheffler, a goalie in recreational ice hockey and roller hockey leagues. "He's like a predator in that he can sense when a team is weakening. Then, that's it. It's over. If you're on his line, all you have to do is have your stick on the ice, and you'll probably have an excellent scoring opportunity."

Many of the items Sheffler owns, Wayne himself might envy. Included in Sheffler's Gretzky collection are a Japanese Upper Deck soccer card, two cards produced in Finland, Indianapolis Racers and Phoenix Roadrunners jerseys worn by Gretzky, a copy of Gretzky's birth certificate, photos of Wayne at 4 days old and Wayne scoring a goal at age 7 — even a *Soviet Life* magazine cover featuring The Great One.

How does Sheffler find all this stuff? Persistence.

"If you're really serious about collecting, you've got to do the legwork, like keeping in touch with companies he represents for promotional items. You also have to think ahead and arrange to get things from significant games," says Sheffler, who credits his friend John Groezinger of St. Louis for helping him kick-start his Gretzky memorabilia collection and build it to where it is today.

Sheffler also keeps up with the vast array of Gretzky memorabilia through a network of six serious Gretzky collectors across the United States and Canada. In 1993, they convened for the first time at a show in Toronto.

"As you can imagine, we had some hellacious trading sessions with a lot of

RON VESELY

Rick's World

Collector extraordinaire Rick Sheffler may not have cornered the market on Wayne Gretzky memorabilia, but he's clearly the king of this particular corner of the hobby

By Timm Boyle

screaming and yelling," Sheffler says. "Nobody got much sleep."

Despite the rivalry, this network of Gretzky collectors provides each other with duplicates and supplies information on hard-to-find items. But even with assistance, it's becoming increasingly difficult to keep up with everything featuring No. 99.

"The real killers are the insert cards," Sheffler says. "[In 1993], counting the inserts, there were about 110 Gretzky cards. I got all of them, but it was expensive.

Sheffler says his most valuable Gretzky collectible is a game-worn, L.A. Kings road jersey worth $9,000, and his most prized item is a game-worn helmet given to him by Gretzky's agent, Michael Barnett, as thanks for Sheffler helping them crack down on unlicensed memorabilia.

Sheffler has met with Gretzky on several occasions, once spending a half-hour with him in the visiting team's dressing room at Chicago Stadium, but he's never asked the superstar for anything. Instead, Sheffler did what any intelligent "courtier" would do: Go through the father.

"I was on my way to a show in Canada with two of my three sons in 1989, and since I knew where his parents lived, I decided to stop by their Brantford [Ontario] house," Sheffler says. "I had some highlight tapes I thought his father would like, and my plan was to give him the stuff and say goodbye.

"But I think Walter liked the fact that I wasn't there to ask for any of Wayne's memorabilia, because he said, 'Where are you going in such a hurry?' We ended up spending almost all day there," Sheffler continues. "Since then, we've kept in touch and exchanged a

Rick Sheffler's world of Wayne Gretzky memorabilia encompasses 2,500 items, from old jerseys to new cards.

lot of Wayne's memorabilia."

Sheffler's Gretzky collection is so extensive that part of it is featured in *Wayne Gretzky: The Authorized Pictorial Biography*, published by Opus Productions Inc. of Vancouver. Needless to say, Sheffler has a copy of the book.

Despite possessing a considerable number of Gretzky collectibles, there always will be something Sheffler is missing. What's the one thing Rick would rather have than anything else?

"If I could have only one hour of Wayne's time," Sheffler says, "to have him come and see my collection would be the ultimate." •

Timm Boyle is a freelance writer in Arlington Heights, Ill.

The Golden

Years

A chronological account of
Wayne Gretzky's 18 seasons of
professional hockey proves that
The Great One truly is the sport's
greatest player ever   By Kevin Allen

1978-79

As a skinny 17-year-old, Wayne Douglas Gretzky began his professional career with the World Hockey Association's Indianapolis Racers. After just eight games, they sold him to the Edmonton Oilers. Despite being named WHA Rookie of the Year after netting 42 goals and 61 assists, NHL scouts still doubted his ability to make it as a pro.

"They said he was too small, too slow," says former Washington and New Jersey executive Max Mc-Nab. "They didn't think he'd survive in the NHL."

BBS

The Oilers joined the NHL and Gretzky shocked most opponents with his uncanny ability to thread passes to open teammates. At 19 years, two months, he became the youngest player to score 50 goals in a season. Although he tied Marcel Dionne for the points lead (137 points), Dionne won the Art Ross Trophy because he had more goals. Gretzky continued to hone his sense of where everyone is on the ice at all times. He often set up behind the net to create scoring chances. Players started calling that spot "Wayne's office."

That summer, the Oilers drafted Paul Coffey in the first round and Jari Kurri in the fourth round. McNab, then with the Capitals, had contemplated taking Kurri earlier in the draft.

"History certainly could have been changed," McNab admits.

1980-81

G retzky is united with Jari Kurri, a Finnish player with speed and an amazing scoring touch, contributing to Wayne's NHL record 164 points and first NHL scoring title. Gretzky was playing with B.J. MacDonald and Brett Callighen before Kurri arrived. Kurri's ability to one-time the puck after feeds from Gretzky made him a perfect fit.

"Their relationship was similar to what law partners enjoy," says Kurri's agent, Don Beizley. "There was a lot of professional respect and admiration and [camaraderie] at work. But you don't necessarily socialize together after work."

Through Gretzky and Kurri's teamwork, Edmonton won its first NHL playoff series upsetting the heavily-favored Montreal Canadiens in the first round.

BBS

BBS

The Great One's 92 goals shattered Phil Esposito's NHL goal-scoring mark by 16. By percentage, the feat is equivalent to someone breaking Roger Maris' home run record by swatting 73 dingers. Gretzky's 61 goals in his first 50 games rank among the most amazing accomplishments of his career. Maurice "Rocket" Richard's record of "50 in 50" stood for 35 years until Mike Bossy tied it in 1980-81. Gretzky also posted single-season records for points (212), assists (120) and hat tricks (10).

1982-83

T he Oilers made the Stanley Cup finals for the first time in their history, but were swept by the Islanders in four games. The defeat had a major impact on The Great One because his father, Walter, the man he ad-mired most, admonished him after Game 4 for not putting forth his maximum effort. He pointed out how his grandmother had worked hard every day of her life. Wayne has reflected on the story often.

BBS

Gretzky and the Oilers gained a measure of revenge as they captured their first Stanley Cup title by knocking off the New York Islanders, the same team that swept Edmonton a year earlier. Hoisting the Stanley Cup trophy for the first time is a memory Gretzky says he'll never forget.

"I remember they said I wasn't a great player until I had won a Cup," Gretzky recalls.

Gretzky began the season with as much success as he ended it. His point scoring streak of 51 consecutive games to start the season was compared to Joe DiMaggio's 56-game hitting streak in baseball. Los Angeles Kings goaltender Markus Mattsson ended the streak by shutting Gretzky out, Jan. 28, 1984. Through the course of the scoring streak, Gretzky accumulated 61 goals and 92 assists.

1984-85

Four of the top five NHL postseason offensive showings belong to Gretzky. His best came in 1984-85 when he registered 47 points en route to the Oilers' second consecutive Stanley Cup title. Gretzky scored 18 points in the conference finals against Chicago. Gretzky claimed his sixth Hart Trophy (MVP), his fifth Art Ross Trophy (scoring leader) and his first Conn Smythe Trophy (playoff MVP).

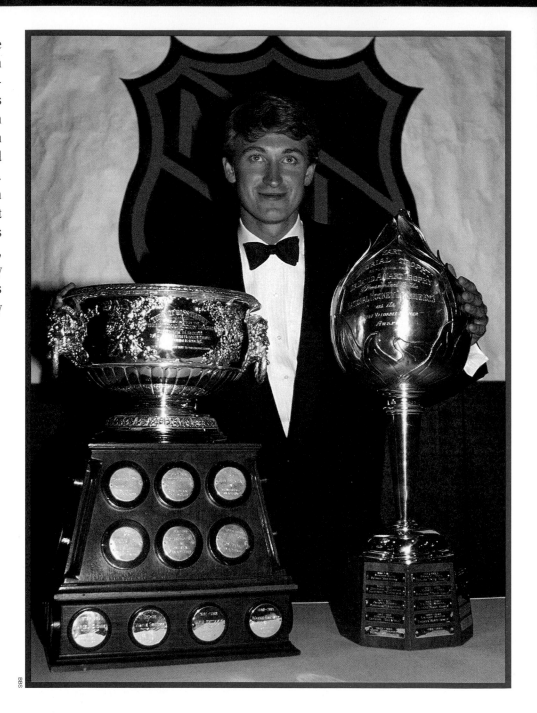

BBS

BBS

S ome thought Gretzky wouldn't be able to top his 92-goal season, but his NHL-record 215 points during the 1985-86 season astounded even those who had come to expect the greatest from him.

"When Wayne sensed the other team was down, he poured it on," said assistant coach John Muckler. "To be a great scorer, you have to take advantage when the other team is at its weakest. Wayne would always do that."

Curiously in his best NHL offensive season, the Oilers flopped in the play-offs, losing to Calgary in the divisional finals.

Gretzky and the Oilers captured their third Stanley Cup title. Gretzky also became the fastest 500-goal scorer in NHL history. In addition, he won his seventh consecutive Art Ross Trophy and his eighth consecutive Hart Trophy.

But all of Gretzky's NHL accomplishments were dwarfed in the wonder of his incredible performance at the '87 Canada Cup tournament. Head coach Mike Keenan moved Mario Lemieux to right wing to play with Gretzky, believing the combination would be too much for the Soviets to handle. Keenan was right. Lemieux scored the game-winning goal with an assist from Gretzky.

"It was great hockey," Gretzky recalls. "And that was probably the best I ever played."

G retzky and the
Oilers re-
mained the
NHL's team-to-beat by winning their fourth Stanley Cup
in five seasons. But owner
Peter Pocklington and general manager Glen Sather
begin to believe Edmonton's
small market can't afford to
pay for all of the team's
high-priced talent.

Gretzky's wedding to
actress Janet Jones that summer is treated like the Royal
Wedding.

"It was like Charles and
Lady Di," says Kings owner
Bruce McNall, who had been
watching the hoopla sur-
rounding Wayne with keen
interest.

At his wedding, Gretzky
tells buddy Paul Coffey that
he expects to be traded.

One month before training camp, Aug. 9, 1988, Wayne Gretzky, Marty McSorley and Mike Krushelnyski are traded to Los Angeles for Jimmy Carson, Martin Gelinas, three first-round picks and $15 million. Gretzky favored the Kings after meeting McNall. The deal immediately is dubbed "The Trade of the Century."

"He deserved the right to choose his own destiny," Oilers owner Peter Pocklington said. "Sometimes your heart says 'no' and your head says 'yes.'"

Wayne's arrival in Los Angeles triggered a hockey explosion in southern California and in the United States.

"When I came back from Canada and saw Wayne Gretzky on *Saturday Night Live* and on billboards in Manhattan, that's when I realized how powerful he really is," said Fox television analyst John Davidson.

BRUCE BENNETT / BBS

BRUCE BENNETT / BBS

On October 15, 1989, Gretzky scored a goal late in the third period at Edmonton to register his 1,851st career point, passing Gordie Howe's record. Later, in a dramatic overtime, Gretzky scored the game-winning goal to beat his former team.

"Everything Wayne did in those days was always big-time," says former Kings teammate Tom Laidlaw. "A tying goal in Edmonton where he had began his ca-reer; that was just so typical of the way Wayne has been throughout his career. When they stopped the game and everyone was cheering, it showed me who he was and what he meant to this game."

With 142 points, Gretzky won his first scoring title since 1986-87. He receives no consideration for MVP.

"He has set such high standards," McNall says. "The problem is there is no other basis for comparison except himself."

The Great One netted his 2,000th point, Oct. 26, at Winnipeg. His continued point production was impressive considering the Kings never really found him any linemates who matched the chemistry he had with Jari Kurri, or even Esa Tikkanen. In his first playoff season as a King, he had Chris Kontos as a winger.

"The joke around the team was [that] at our farm team in New Haven, they ran a regular contest with the winner getting two tickets to Disneyland and a chance to play as Wayne's wing," former Kings owner Bruce McNall said.

Comedy aside, the Kings produced an impressive 46-24-10 record and advanced as far as the Division finals before losing to Edmonton.

B. MILLER / BBS

STEVE REYES / BBS

With his 732nd career goal coming on Dec. 21, 1991, against Detroit, Gretzky passed Marcel Dionne for second place on the NHL's all-time list. At 30, Gretzky moved off his early prediction of retiring when he was 30 or 31.

"When I was 20, like most 20-year-olds in all sports, I talked like that," Gretzky says. "Then you reach 29 and 30 and you think you want to play as long as you can."

Although Gretzky continued to flourish as an individual, the Kings struggled. L.A. bowed out of the playoffs in the first round, again, to Gretzky's old team, the Edmonton Oilers.

1992-93

The 1992-93 season marked the best of times and worst of times for Gretzky. Although he had missed just 41 games in his previous 13 NHL seasons, The Great One was sidelined 39 games with a herniated disk. However, when he returned from the injury, he helped propel the Kings to their first Stanley Cup final in team history. During the conference finals against Toronto, the media suggested he wasn't playing as well as he had in the past. He immediately responded by scoring the overtime winner in Game 6 and netting a hat trick in Game 7.

"He's always turned negatives into positive motivation," says Mike Barnett, his long-time agent and friend.

The Kings lost to Montreal in the finals, but Gretzky finished with 40 points in the playoffs. Still, 15 minutes after the loss, Gretzky said he was considering retirement.

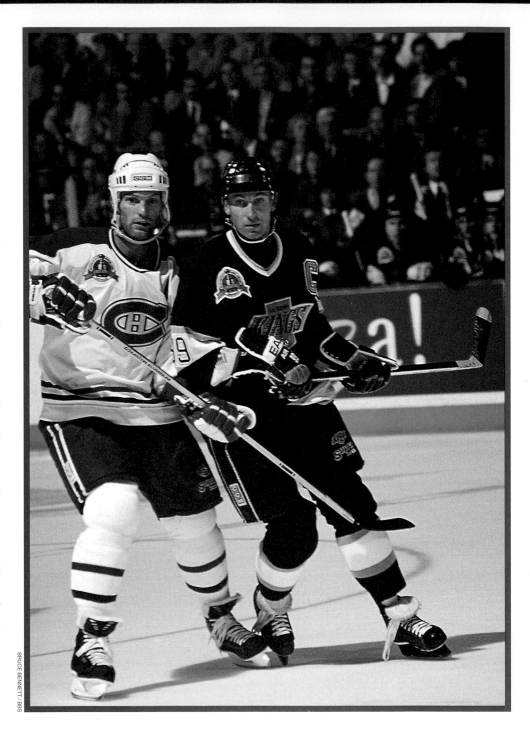

BRUCE BENNETT / BBS

BRUCE BENNETT / BBS

Refreshed and feeling healthy, Gretzky returned to the ice. And on March 22, 1994, he scored his 802nd career NHL goal to pass Howe and become the NHL's all-time leading goal scorer. Howe held the scoring record for 30 years and four months. Gretzky said he had mixed emotions about passing Howe, whom he idolizes. He says the best advice he ever received in hockey came from Howe.

"When I was 17, Gordie told me: 'You've got two ears and only one mouth. That's for a reason.' "

In the ceremony to highlight the milestone, commissioner Gary Bettman said, "Wayne, you've always been great, but tonight you've become the greatest."

When collective bargaining talks stalled at the beginning of the 1994-95 season, NHL owners locked the players out. With the NHL shut down, Gretzky assembled a group of NHL All-Stars for a European exhibition tour. For the Europeans, it was like an NHL all-star game with each stop on the tour. For NHL fans in North America, they could only wait and hope the lockout would soon end.

By mid-January, a settlement finally had been reached and the NHL resumed play. But things may have been more enjoyable for Gretzky when he was overseas. The Kings finished fifth in their Pacific Division with a 27-45-12 record and Gretzky missed the playoffs for the first time in his career.

BBS

With McNall no longer the owner and the Kings not destined to make the playoffs, Gretzky said in January that it was "probably best" for him and the franchise that he be traded. So on Feb. 27, the Kings traded Gretzky to St. Louis.

Blues president Jack Quinn said bringing in The Great One to play with Brett Hull is like "bringing in Mickey Mantle to play with Roger Maris."

But the honeymoon turned sour quickly. In the playoffs, Blues general manager and head coach Mike Keenan berated Gretzky in front of his teammates and then publicly raised questions when he said, "If he's not injured, then something must be bothering him."

Gretzky also was concerned about trade rumors involving Hull. Through it all, Gretzky still managed 102 points, the 16th 100-point season of his career. •

Kevin Allen covers hockey for the USA Today.

STORY BY JACK DEVRIES

PENCILS BY RICHARD DOMINGUEZ

INKS BY RICHARD DOMINGUEZ

COLOR BY OMAR MEDIANO AND
MARK STOKES

LETTERING BY JOHN MARSHALL

STORY CONSULTANT:
RUDY J. KLANCNIK

EDITOR: FRED L. REED III

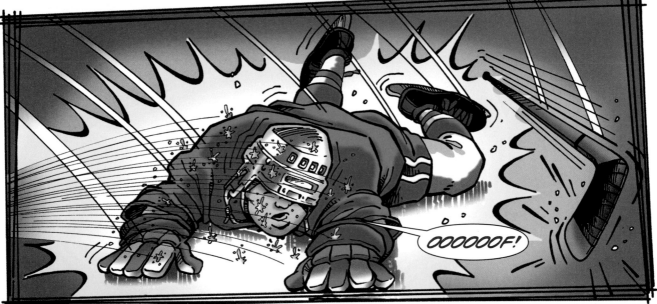

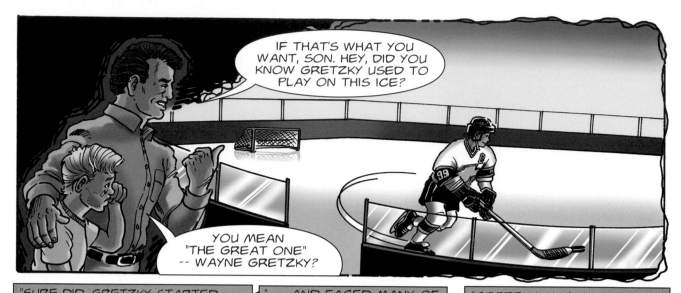

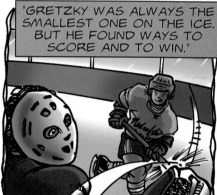

"GRETZKY WAS SKATING AT AGE 2 AND PLAYING HOCKEY SOON AFTER. HIS FATHER WOULD FLOOD THEIR BACKYARD AND BUILD WAYNE AN OUTDOOR RINK EACH WINTER."

C'MON, WAYNE, FASTER! THAT'S IT!

"HIS FATHER DEVISED MANY DRILLS -- EVEN HAD WAYNE SHOOTING PUCKS THROUGH THE SLATS IN THEIR PICNIC TABLE INTO THE NET."

CLOSE, SON, TRY ANOTHER ONE.

"BY 6, WAYNE WAS IN HIS FIRST ORGANIZED HOCKEY LEAGUE PLAYING AGAINST 10-YEAR-OLDS."

NOT SO FAST, PAL!

"AND WHILE GRETZKY MAY HAVE BEEN SMALLER . . ."

GET THE LITTLE-- AGGHHH!

C'MERE, YOU-- NOOOO!

". . . HIS DETERMINATION TO SUCCEED WAS GREATER THAN ANY OPPONENT."

"BY 1979, WAYNE GRETZKY WAS 18 YEARS OLD AND IN THE NHL . . ."

"WHERE THE PLAYERS ARE NOT ONLY BIG . . ."

". . .THEY'RE THE BEST IN THE WORLD."

"GRETZKY WAS AN INCREDIBLE SCORER AND AWARD WINNER DURING HIS EARLY YEARS IN THE LEAGUE . . ."

BUT TO BE TRULY GREAT, HE HAD TO HELP HIS TEAM WIN THE STANLEY CUP . . .

"TO WIN THE CUP, THEY'D HAVE TO TAKE IT FROM THE NEW YORK ISLANDERS -- MONSTERS OF THE NHL!"

"MONSTERS!?"

"YES, MONSTERS . . .THE LAST NHL DYNASTY, WINNERS OF FOUR STRAIGHT CUPS AND TERRORS ON THE ICE. IT WOULD BE GRETZKY'S GREATEST CHALLENGE."

"THE ISLANDERS THREW EVERY WEAPON THEY HAD AT GRETZKY, AND STILL HE WAS ABLE TO TRIUMPH AND HELP THE EDMONTON OILERS WIN THEIR FIRST STANLEY CUP."

BLZZPP!

WHOK!

ZWIPP!

FWOOSH!

KRUNCH!

GRETZKY WENT ON TO WIN MORE STANLEY CUPS, SET RECORDS AND WIN TONS OF AWARDS.

HE NEVER WAS THE FASTEST, BIGGEST OR STRONGEST PLAYER IN ANY SEASON --ONLY THE BEST.

I THINK I'LL GIVE HOCKEY ANOTHER TRY TOMORROW. I'LL START PRACTICING HARDER. NOBODY'S GOING TO RUN ME OFF THE ICE.

BUT I SURE HOPE THOSE MONSTERS WAYNE PLAYED AGAINST HAVE ALL RETIRED BY THE TIME I GET TO THE NHL.

END

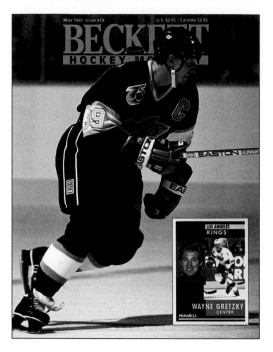

the enduring appeal of The Great One, as well as the accompanying story on his collecting interests, prompted his appearance on the cover of *BHM* issue #19 (May 1992).

gretzky's record-breaking 802nd career goal was the occasion for his most recent and, fittingly, record fourth appearance on a *BHM* cover in issue #42 (April 1994).

for hockey fans, it's a terrible question. What if there were no Wayne Gretzky?

For starters, chances are hockey popularity never would have skyrocketed in the United States. Without Gretzky, maybe a hockey magazine in Dallas, the heart of football country, never would have been imagined. The NHL record book would have an entirely different look to it, and a generation of hockey fans would have been deprived of the skill and imagination he brought to the game.

Anyone who has witnessed The Great One's artistry on ice can appreciate the treatments Gretzky has received on the covers and in the pages of *Beckett Hockey Monthly* throughout the years. It's impossible to forget Wayne's contributions to hockey. "Beckett® Remembers" sure doesn't.

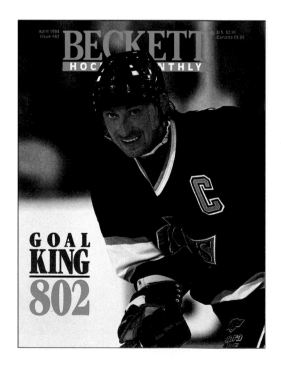

beckett®

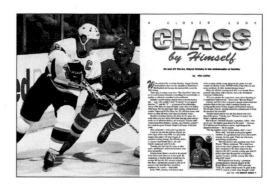

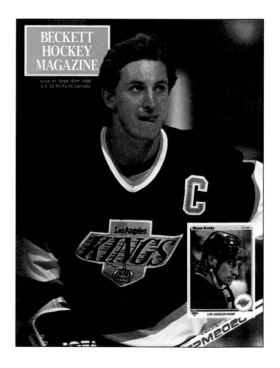

wayne has been No. 1 with us and in a "Class by Himself" with our readers since we chose him as the cover subject for the premiere issue of *BHM* (September/ October 1990).

rob MacDougall's inspired cover art-work of Gretzky helped us celebrate *BHM's* 25th issue (November 1992).

remembers

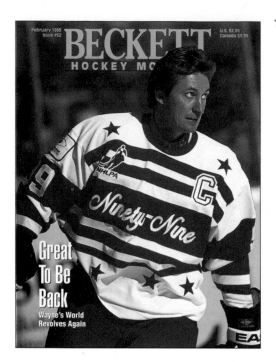

February 1995
Issue #52

BECKETT
HOCKEY MO

U.S. $2.95
Canada $3.95

Great
To Be
Back

Wayne's World
Revolves Again

beckett

gretzky
played his final game for the L.A. Kings on Feb. 27, 1996 at Winnipeg. His last appearance in *BHM* as a King came via Tim Cortes' artwork in issue #64 (February 1996).

during the lockout of the 1994-95 season, Gretzky and a few of his NHL friends participated in a tour of exhibition games overseas (*BHM* #52, February, 1995).

remembers

with a change in scenery, Gretzky continued to shine in the spotlight, leading his new team to a near upset in the playoffs over the heavily-favored Red Wings. Opie Otterstad supplied artwork depicting Gretzky in his new colors for the front cover of *BHM #66* (April 1996).

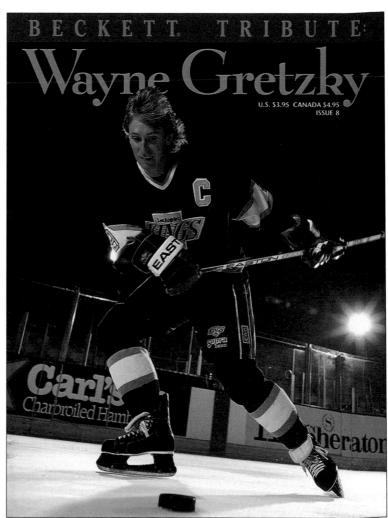

following the 1993-94 season — the one in which Gretzky supplanted Gordie Howe as the NHL's all-time leading goal scorer — Beckett Publications honored The Great One with *Beckett Tribute: Wayne Gretzky.*

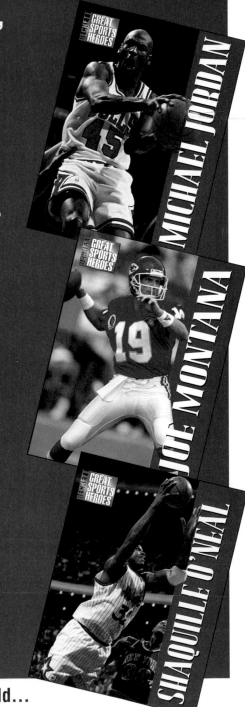